Reasoning Olympiad

Class 04

Reasoning Olympiad

Class 04

A must have book for all
Olympiads & Talent Search Exams...

by
Prachi

BLOOM CAP
Bloom Cap Edu Ventures Pvt. Ltd.

Bloom Cap Edu Ventures Pvt. Ltd.

☸ **Administrative & Production Office**

'Ramchhaya' 4577/15, Agarwal Road, Darya Ganj, New Delhi -110002
Tele: 011- 47630600, 43518550

☸ **ISBN :** 978-93-25519-03-9

☸ **PRICE :** ₹100.00

☸ **PO No :** TXT-XX-XXXXXXX-X-XX

For further information about the books log on to
www.bloomcap.org

Follow us on   

Preface

"Future belongs to those Who prepares for it today"

School Olympiads are National & International level competitions conducted by different Government, Non-Government & Educational Organisations with the purpose of making the children ready to face competitive exams. The challenging Questions asked in Olympiads motivate them to learn more & more and bring out the best result with improved academic performance. The Awards & Scholarship offered by Olympiads motivate children to aspire & strive for doing better and emerge out to be the best.

Reasoning Olympiads

Reasoning or Logical thinking is the ability of mind that helps in dealing with complex situations. It is also directly related to evolving careers like Software Development, Coding, Mobile App Development etc.

Reasoning Olympiads are targeted to induce & enhance the logical thinking skills and Analytical Approach in students which further aid to improve their academics.

'Bloom Reasoning Olympiad Study Book Class 4' is a perfect resource to Study & Practice for Olympiad Exams and other National & State Level Talent Search Exams & Other Competitions.

Some Special Features of Bloom Reasoning Olympiad Study Books are;

- Complete coverage of all the aspects of Reasoning; Verbal, Non-Verbal, Analytical & Logical Reasoning etc.
- Chapterwise Exercises having different types of Objective Questions at par with the Olympiad Level.
- Detailed Explanation for each question.
- Olympiad Pattern Practice Sets at the end.

This book is prepared by Expert Panel with the utmost care, still if you have any suggestions regarding its improvement then feel free to contact us at olympiads@bloomcap.org. We will try to inculcate your suggestions in the further editions.

Contents

Matching Pairs

'Matching pairs' means to find the similarity between two pairs.
In 'Matching Pairs', following types of questions are generally asked.

EXAMPLE 1 In the given figures the first pair is related to each other in a certain way. Find the figure which will complete the second pair in the same way as in the first pair.

Sol. *(c)* As, in the first pair of figures, a shaded square is drawn inside the square to obtain the second figure. Similarly, in second pair, a shaded circle is to be drawn inside the circle to obtain the second figure. Hence, option (c) is correct.

EXAMPLE 2 Which number from the given alternatives will replace the question mark (?)?

    (a) 12   (b) 24   (c) 6   (d) 16

Sol. *(d)* As, $24 \xrightarrow{\div 3} 8$ Similarly, $48 \xrightarrow{\div 3} \boxed{16}$ Hence, option (d) is correct.

EXAMPLE 3 Find the letters from the given alternatives that would be written on the last box following the same pattern as used in the first pair.

    AC : BD :: TV : ?

    (a) YZ   (b) XY   (c) UW   (d) WU

Sol. *(c)* As, $\begin{matrix} A & C \\ {\scriptstyle +1}\downarrow & {\scriptstyle +1}\downarrow \\ B & D \end{matrix}$ Similarly, $\begin{matrix} T & V \\ {\scriptstyle +1}\downarrow & {\scriptstyle +1}\downarrow \\ \boxed{U\ W} \end{matrix}$

Hence, option (c) is correct.

EXAMPLE 4 Complete the second pair in the same way as the first pair.
Snake is to Reptile in the same way as whale is to

    (a) Pisces   (b) Mammal

    (c) Aves   (d) Insect

Sol. As, snake is a reptile. Similarly, whale is a mammal.
    Hence, option (b) is correct.

Matching Pairs Based on Alphabet

In such type of questions, the letters of English alphabet are related to numbers using some properties of the letters like sum, product, place value, Reverse place value or some other method to form the analogy.

> **Note** Following table showing letters position in English alphabetical series will help the students to solve these type of questions.

Forward	1	2	3	4	5	6	7	8	9	10	11	12	13	14	15	16	17	18	19	20	21	22	23	24	25	26
Alphabet	A	B	C	D	E	F	G	H	I	J	K	L	M	N	O	P	Q	R	S	T	U	V	W	X	Y	Z
Backward	26	25	24	23	22	21	20	19	18	17	16	15	14	13	12	11	10	9	8	7	6	5	4	3	2	1

Let us consider the following examples

EXAMPLE 5 Which number from the given alternative will replace the question mark ?

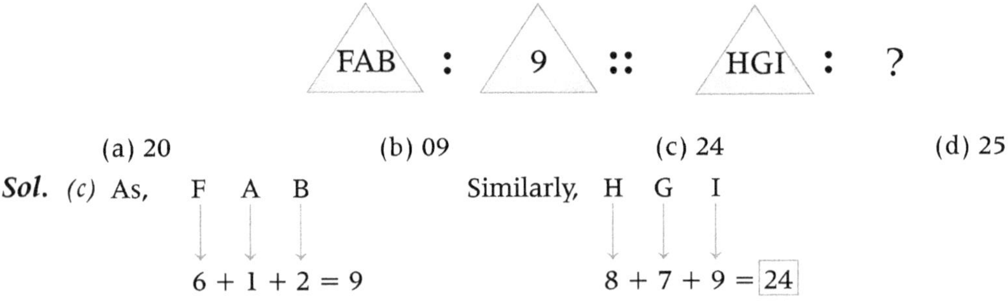

    (a) 20   (b) 09   (c) 24   (d) 25

Sol. *(c)* As,   F   A   B   Similarly, H   G   I

            $6 + 1 + 2 = 9$ $8 + 7 + 9 = \boxed{24}$

Hence, option (c) is correct.

EXAMPLE 6 Patlu is a naughty boy. So he write word 'RICE' which is related to '18935' in a certain way to tease him friend, Motu to understand. Help Motu to find out how can he write word 'PRICE'.

    (a) 1618539   (b) 1618953

    (c) 1681935   (d) 1618935

Sol. *(d)* Here, in the given word, every letter has been given its alphabetical position number.

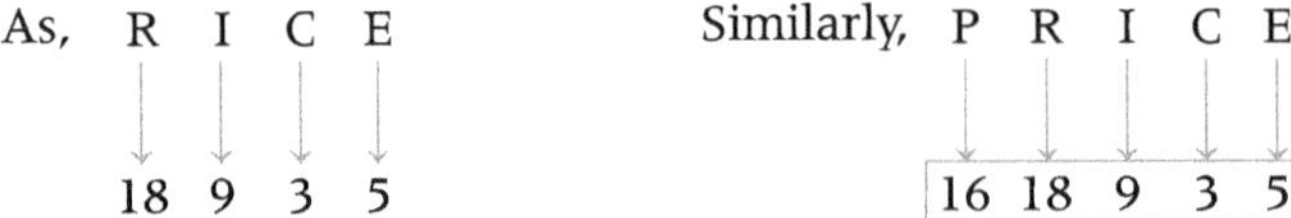

Hence, option (d) is correct.

Let's Practice

1. Find the figure that would complete the second pair in the same way as the first pair.

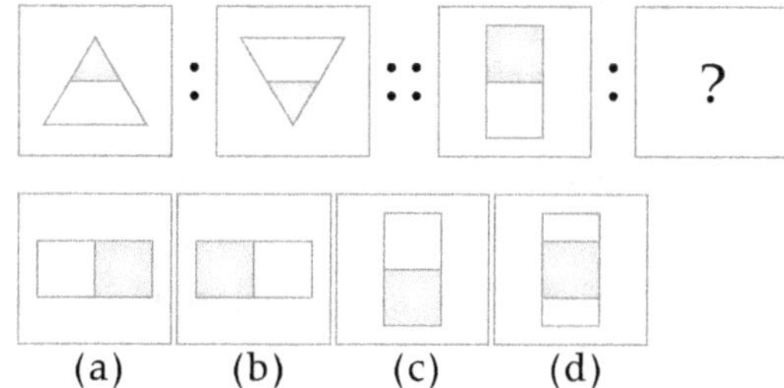

   (a)   (b)   (c)   (d)

2. Which figure will complete the second pair in the same way as the first pair?

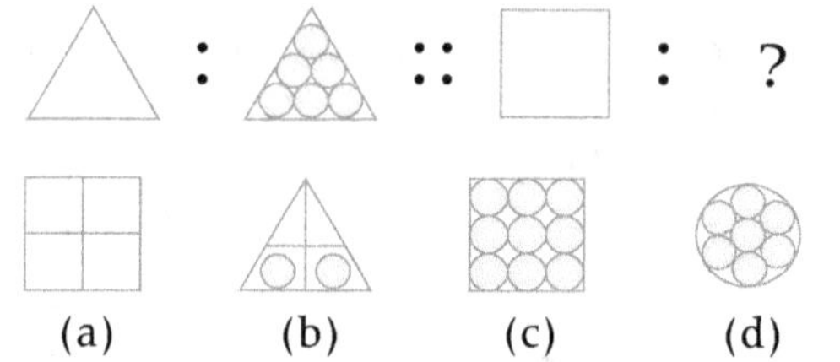

   (a)   (b)   (c)   (d)

3. Which pattern from the given alternatives will complete the given set of patterns in the same way as the patterns in the first pair?

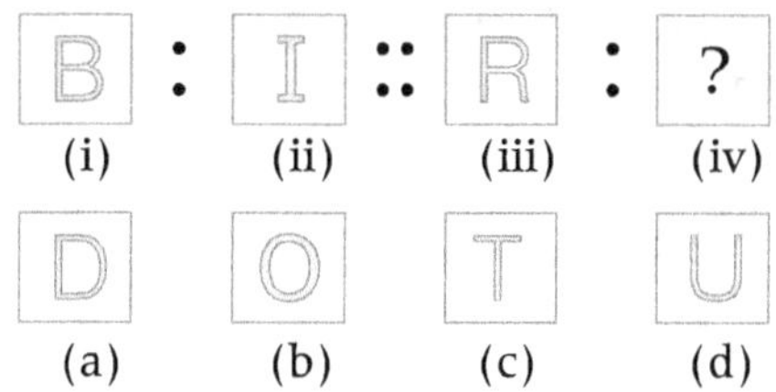

   (a)   (b)   (c)   (d)

4. Which figure will replace the question mark (?)?

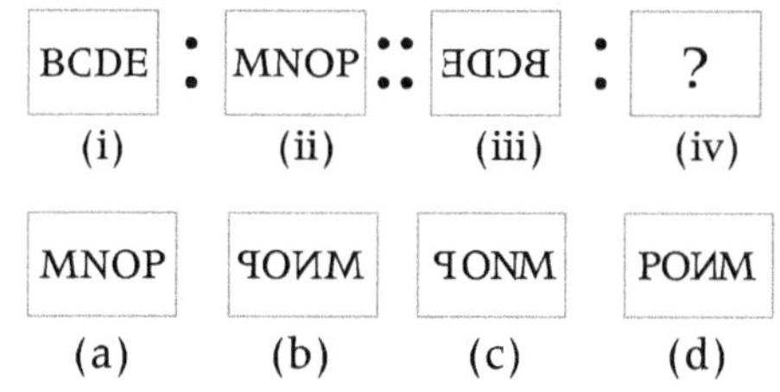

   (a)   (b)   (c)   (d)

5. Some numbers are written on the stickers and they are related to each other in a certain way. Find the number which will be on the last sticker following the same pattern as the first two follow.

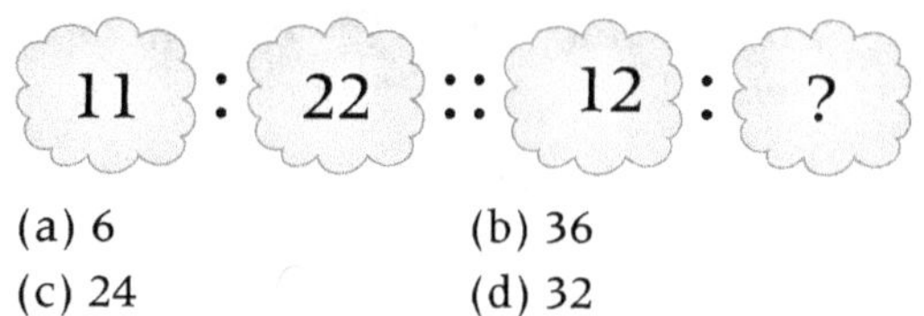

(a) 6   (b) 36
(c) 24   (d) 32

6. A child corelates the numbers on the tambola coins with each other as shown below. Find the number on the last coin that will be related to third coin in the same way as the first two are related.

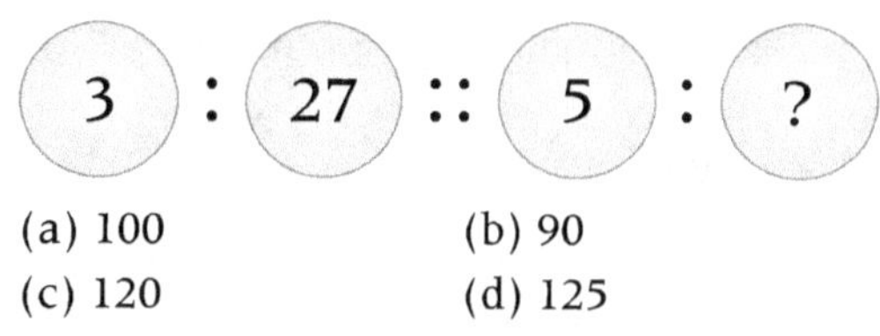

(a) 100   (b) 90
(c) 120   (d) 125

7. Find the number from the given alternatives that would replace the question mark (?) following the pattern which first two numbers follow.

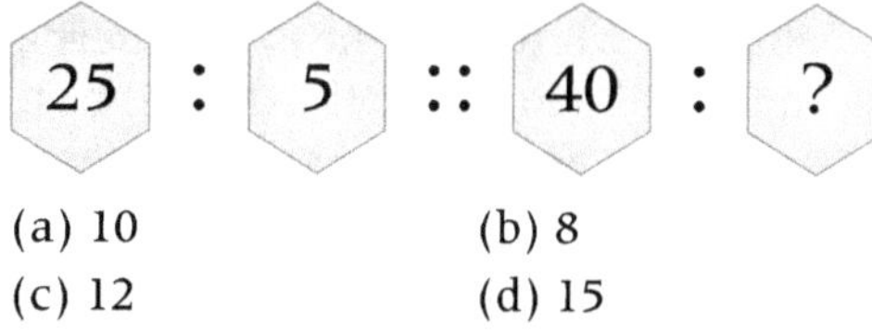

(a) 10   (b) 8
(c) 12   (d) 15

8. Numbers on the first and second tickets are related to each other in a certain way. Similarly, numbers on the third and fourth tickets are related. Find the number on the last ticket.

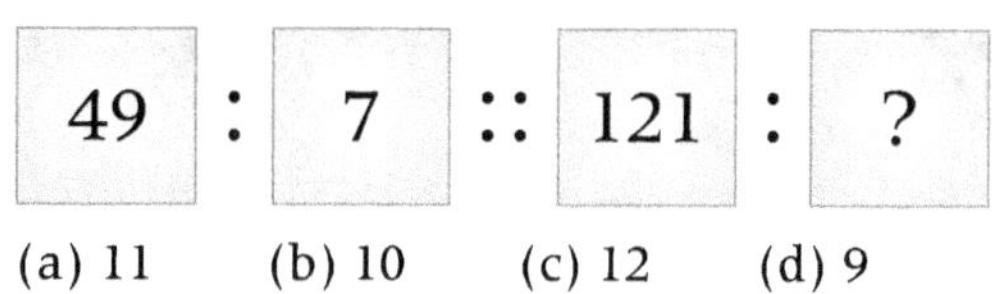

(a) 11   (b) 10   (c) 12   (d) 9

9. Complete the second pair in the same way as first pair.

   389 : 8 :: 462 : ?

   (a) 4 (b) 16 (c) 6 (d) 2

10. Some letters are written on a key on both sides and they are related to each other in a certain way. Find the letters that will be related to the letters on the other key in the same way as the first two are related.

    BA : FE :: LK : ?

    (a) PO (b) OR (c) QR (d) ST

11. Which group of letters from the given alternatives will replace the question mark following the pattern that first pair follows?

    XTV : UQS :: PMQ : ?

    (a) JKM   (b) NMJ
    (c) MJN   (d) LMO

12. Which word is related to the third word in the same way as the first two words are related.

    Sword : Warrior :: Pen : ?

    (a) Writer   (b) Player
    (c) Painter   (d) Engineer

13. Find the word from the given alternatives that is related to the third word in the same way as the first two are related to each other.

    Coffee : Seeds : : Tea : ?

    (a) Hot   (b) Leaves
    (c) Tree   (d) Strong

14. KTM is related to NRN in the same way as IR is related to

    (a) LPW   (b) PLW
    (c) JSX   (d) HTX

15. FH is related to DF as UY is related to

    (a) SW   (b) TX
    (c) RX   (d) TW

16. ABC is related to CBA as QMP is related to

    (a) MPQ   (b) MQP
    (c) QPM   (d) PMQ

17. Eat is to Heat as Arm is to

    (a) Farm   (b) Harm
    (c) Warm   (d) Tarm

18. Complete the given set of words following the same pattern as followed by first two words.

    Pear is to Fruit as Spinach is to

    (a) Grain   (b) Salad
    (c) Vegetable   (d) Root

19. Exercise is related to Gym as Eating is related to

    (a) Drinking   (b) Dieting
    (c) Fitness   (d) Restaurant

20. Shaurya is a creative boy. He write the word 'LION' which is related to '04' in a certain way. Find out how he write the word 'TIGER' with the same creativity?

    (a) 04   (b) 06
    (c) 07   (d) 05

21. Parul has a habit of forgetting. So she write the word 'India' which is related to '25' in a certain way. How she write the word 'NAGALAND' in a similar way, so, she could remember.

    (a) 36   (b) 49
    (c) 64   (d) 25

22. In a certain way 'MEERA' is related to 1355181. In a same way how 'MADHAV' can be written?

    (a) 13418122   (b) 13148122
    (c) 13411823   (d) 13411824

Odd One Out

'Odd one out' means picking out the thing/item which is different from others in a group. To understand the concept of 'odd one out', let us discuss the following example.

EXAMPLE 1 Which one is different ?

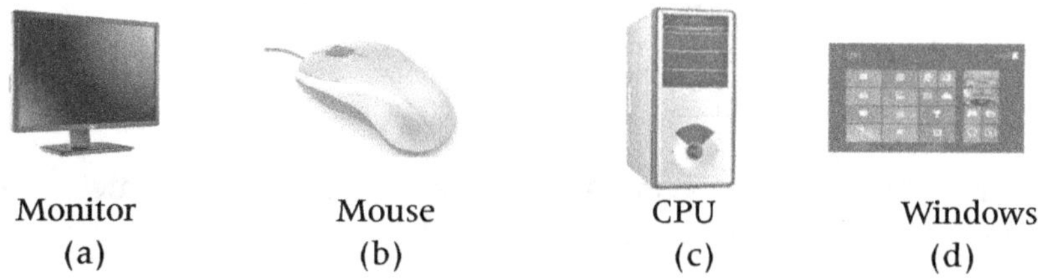

Monitor	Mouse	CPU	Windows
(a)	(b)	(c)	(d)

Sol. (d) In the given pictures, Monitor, Mouse and CPU are hardware devices, while windows is a software. Thus, windows is different from others. Hence, option (d) is correct.

EXAMPLE 2 Children drew some shapes on the drawing sheets, which are as shown below. Find the one which is different.

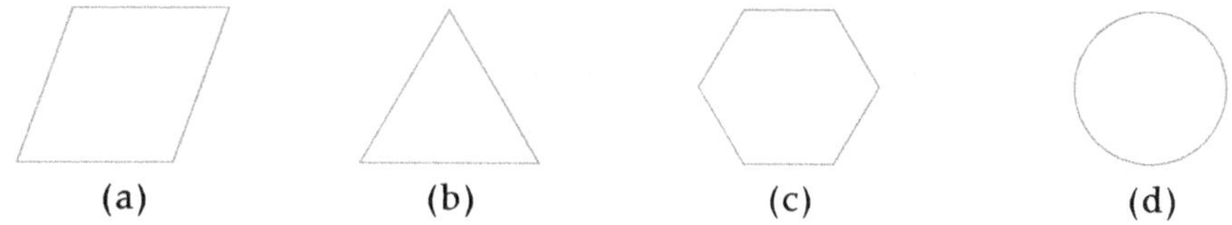

(a)	(b)	(c)	(d)

Sol. (d) All the shapes are made up of lines except figure in option (d).
So, option figure (d) is different from others. Hence, option (d) is correct.

EXAMPLE 3 Which house number is different from others?

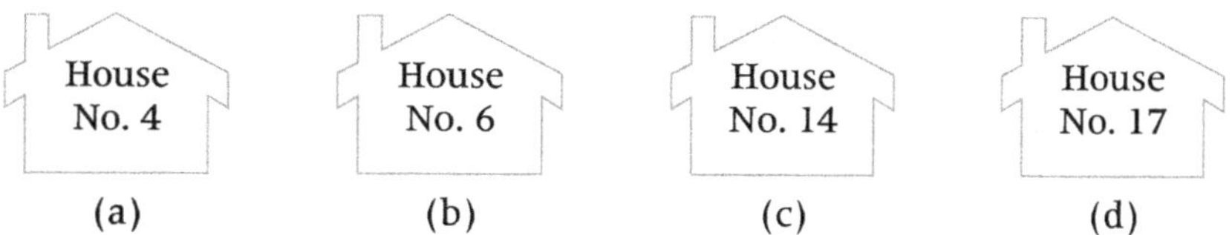

(a)	(b)	(c)	(d)

Sol. (d) All except house number '17' are even numbers. So, 17 is different from others. Hence, option (d) is correct.

EXAMPLE 4   Which letter does not fit into the group?

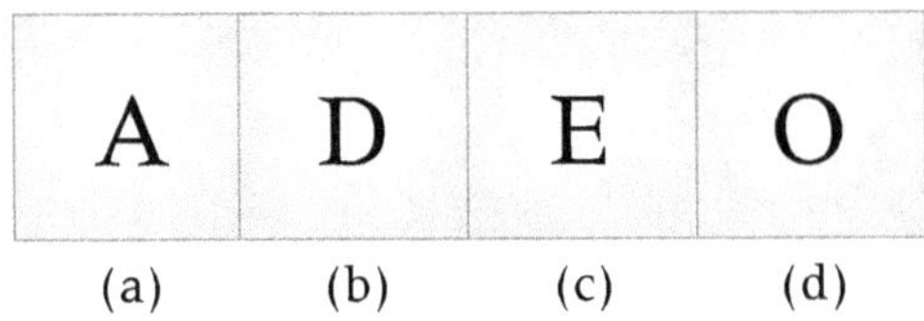

(a)   (b)   (c)   (d)

Sol. *(b)* All the letters except 'D' are vowels, while 'D' is a consonant. So, 'D' does not fit into the group. Hence, option (b) is correct.

EXAMPLE 5   Four students have been given four different things that are shown below. Find the odd one from amongst them.

Pencil	Pen	Table	Eraser
(a)	(b)	(c)	(d)

Sol. *(c)* Pencil, pen and eraser are stationery items while table is a furniture. So, it is different among all others. Hence, option (c) is correct.

EXAMPLE 6   In the following question, four pairs of words are given, out of which three pairs bear a certain common relationship. Choose the pair in which the words are differently related.

(a) Petrol : car   (b) Ink : Pen

(c) Garbage : Dustbin   (d) Head : Pencil

Sol. *(d)* Except option (d), in all others, first is required by the second for its functioning. Hence, option (d) is correct.

EXAMPLE 7   As cup is related to coffee in the same way bowl is related to?

(a) Dish   (b) Soup

(c) Spoon   (d) Food

Sol. *(b)* As, coffee goes into a cup similarly, soup goes into a bowl.

⏰ Let's Practice

1. In Kartik's birthday party, children wore the birthday caps which are shown below. Find the one which looks different from others.

(a) 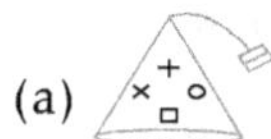 (b) 

(c) 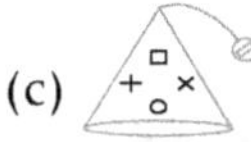 (d) 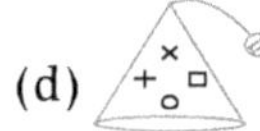

2. Which picture is different from among the following?

(a) 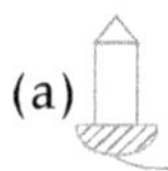 (b) 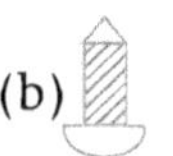 (c) 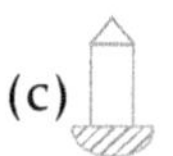 (d) 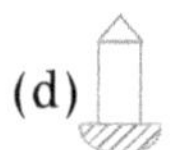

3. Choose the odd one out from the group of figures.

(a) 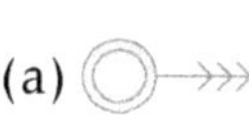 (b) 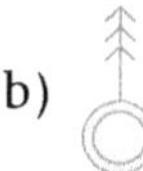

(c)  (d) 

4. Which one of the given figures is different?

(a)  (b) 

(c)  (d) 

5. Find odd one out?

(a) 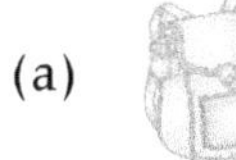 (b) 

(c)  (d) 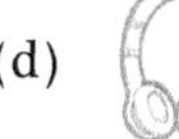

6. Select the odd one out?

(a) 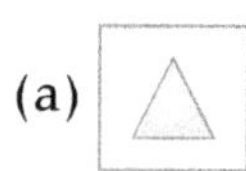 (b) 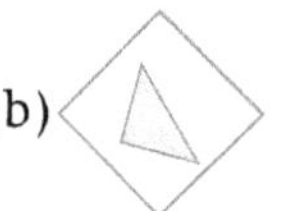

(c)  (d) 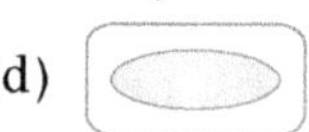

7. Which figure is different from the others?

(a)  (b) 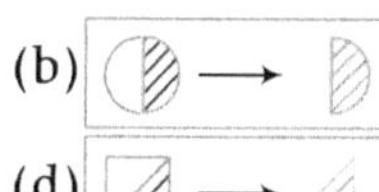

(c) 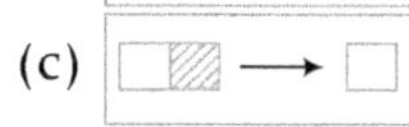 (d) 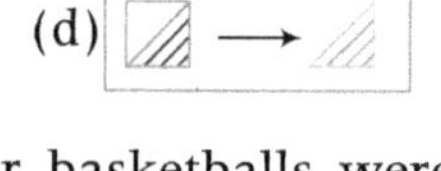

8. In a sports room, four basketballs were kept. Hardik went to the sports room and choose a basketball which was different from others. Which basketball did Hardik choose?

(a) 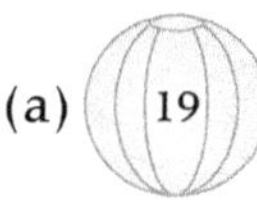 (b) 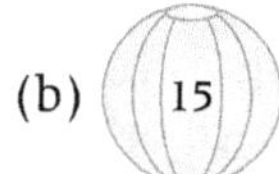

(c) 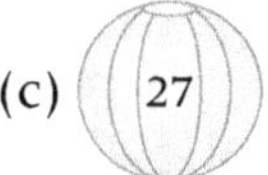 (d) 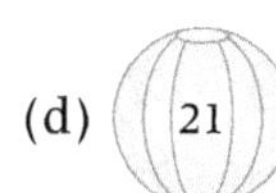

9. In a football team, four players wore the t-shirt having different numbers on it. From amongst them, find the one which is different.

(a) 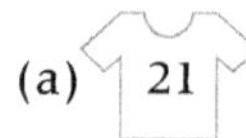 21 (b) 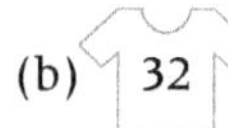 32 (c) 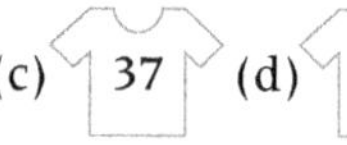 37 (d) 15

10. Find the number which is different from others in this rectangle.

4	36	444
8	27	28
12	16	100
48	888	52
1000	24	32

(a) 27   (b) 72   (c) 888   (d) 100

11. Select the odd one out?

(a) 16 (b) 09

(c) 23 (d) 36

12. Find the number which is different from others.
(a) 182 (b) 824
(c) 236 (d) 345

13. Choose the letter which is different in the group.

(a) T (b) D

(c) R (d) P

14. Choose the odd pair of letters.
(a) BD (b) CE
(c) FH (d) NL

15. Find the pair of letters which is different from others.

(a) BY (b) IR

(c) NP (d) LO

16. Choose the odd pair of letters.
(a) JKL (b) GHI
(c) OPQ (d) ILT

17. Choose the odd one out.
(a) GTB (b) TBT
(c) SZF (d) UPS

18. Choose the odd one out.
(a) ERs (b) PtK
(c) MiG (d) cvZ

19. Which word does not belong with the others?
(a) Noun (b) Preposition
(c) Punctuation (d) Adverb

20. Choose the musical instrument which is different from others.
(a) Violin (b) Sitar
(c) Guitar (d) Piano

21. Find the month which is different from others.
(a) March (b) May
(c) June (d) October

22. Find the odd one out from the following.
(a) Cardamom (b) Turmeric
(c) Sugar (d) Clove

23. In a Science book, parts of body were written. A student while reading them picked out a part of body which he thinks is odd in the group. Find the one which he would have picked out.
(a) Eye (b) Bone
(c) Ear (d) Hand

Directions (Q. Nos. 24 and 25) In each of the following questions, certain pairs of words are given, out of which the words in all pairs except one, bear a certain common relationship. Choose the odd pair.

24. (a) Inkpot : Ink
(b) Cup : Tea
(c) Pitcher : Water
(d) Ball : Bat

25. (a) Shirt : Dress
(b) Boy : Girl
(c) Mango : Fruit
(d) Table : Furniture

What Comes Next?

Series is a continuous sequence of figures, Numbers and Alphabets that follow some defined rule. To understand the concept of 'What comes next?', Let us first consider the following type of examples

EXAMPLE 1 Joe made this pattern.

What comes next in this pattern?

Sol. *(a)* The pictures follow a pattern in which first and second pictures appear again on sixth and seventh position and again in place of question mark first picture will come, so a pattern is formed.
Hence, option (a) is correct.

EXAMPLE 2 The teacher, on the board drew the certain geometrical shapes in which number of sides increases by one. Which shape will come next in the pattern?

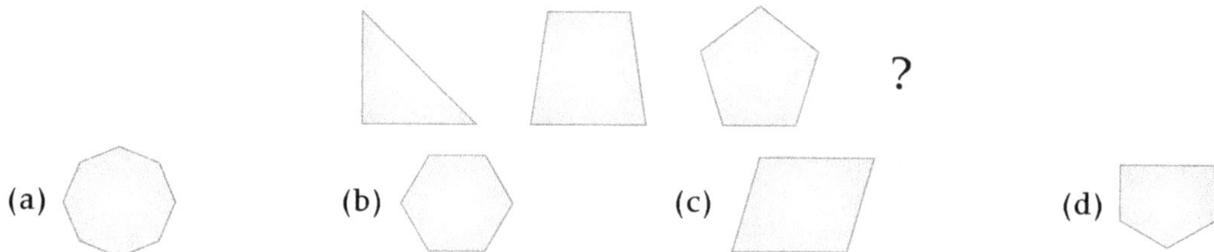

Sol. *(b)* In the question, the number of sides of the first figure is increased by one to get the second and one side is added to the second to get the third. Similarly, one side will be added in the third figure to get the figure given in option (b).
Hence, option (b) is correct.

EXAMPLE 3 What would come in place of question mark (?) ?

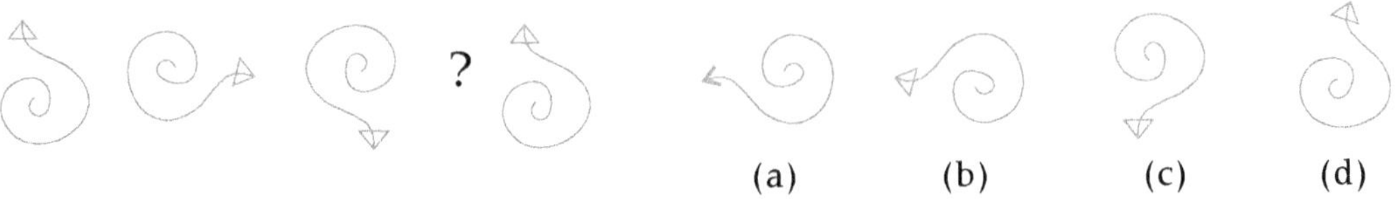

(a)   (b)   (c)   (d)

Sol. *(b)* In the above sets of figures, the figures are rotating one fourth step in clockwise direction to get the next figure. Hence, option (b) is correct.

EXAMPLE 4 Observe the pattern in first three figures and calculate the number of mangoes in the fifth figure.

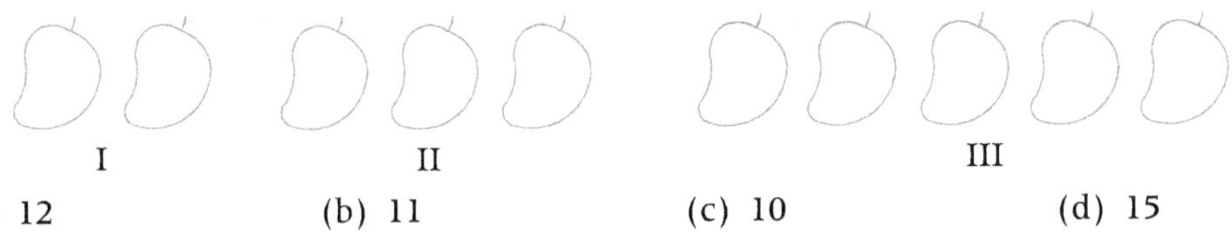

I   II   III

(a) 12   (b) 11   (c) 10   (d) 15

Sol. *(a)* The pattern is I→ 2, II→ 2 + 1 = 3, III→ 3 + 2 = 5, IV→ 5 + 3 = 8, V→ 8 + 4 = 12

So, fifth figure will contain '12' mangoes. Hence, option (a) is correct.

EXAMPLE 5 Four friends were playing a game in which each one has to pick up a chit. One friend picked up the chit but the number was missing on that. What could be the number on that chit if it follows a table of '5'?

| 5 | 10 | ? | 20 |

(a) 25   (b) 12   (c) 15   (d) 17

Sol. *(c)* The pattern is $5 \times 2 = 10, 5 \times 3 = \boxed{15}, \ 5 \times 4 = 20$

So, the missing chit number is '15'. Hence, option (c) is correct.

EXAMPLE 6 What will be the name of hut number 3 ?

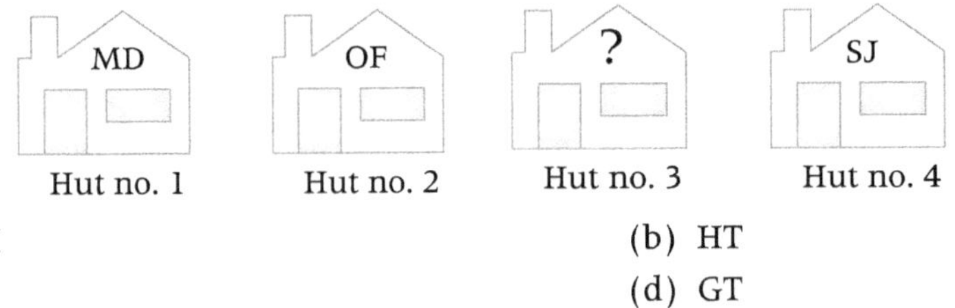

Hut no. 1   Hut no. 2   Hut no. 3   Hut no. 4

(a) QH   (b) HT

(c) TQ   (d) GT

Sol. *(a)* The pattern is as follows :

Ist series, $M \xrightarrow{+2} O \xrightarrow{+2} Q \xrightarrow{+2} S$

IInd series, $D \xrightarrow{+2} F \xrightarrow{+2} H \xrightarrow{+2} J$

So, 'QH' will be the name of hut number 3. Hence, option (a) is correct.

⏰ Let's Practice

1. Which one of the following figures will continue the series?

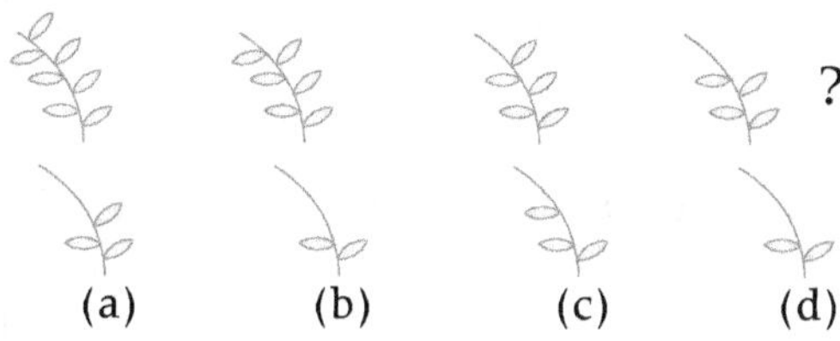

(a)   (b)   (c)   (d)

2. What will come in place of question mark (?) ?

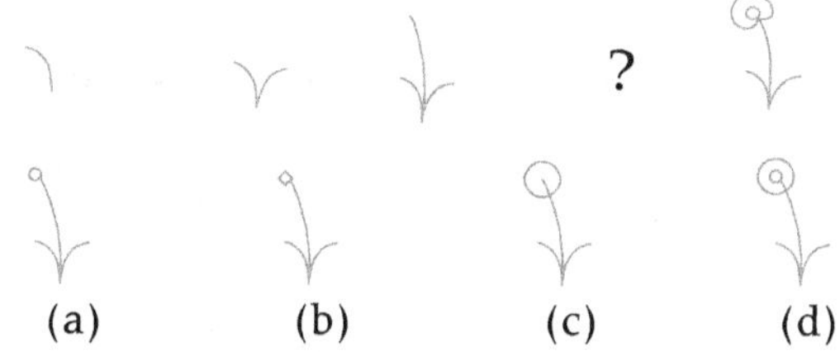

(a)   (b)   (c)   (d)

3. Which figure will replace the question mark (?)?

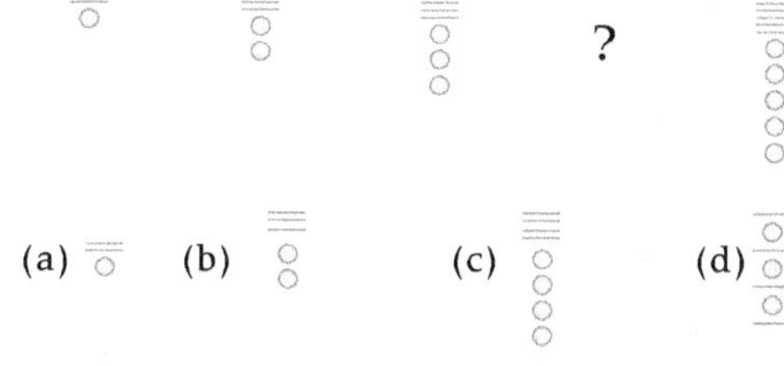

(a)   (b)   (c)   (d)

4. Which answer figures will continue the sequence ?

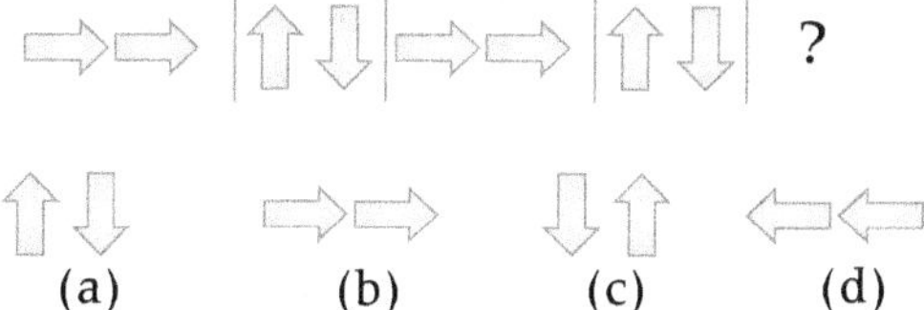

(a)   (b)   (c)   (d)

5. Which figure is the missing figure of the sequence?

6. Five children are playing a game with a block attached with an arrow. Whenever they passes the block from one person to the another, the block and the arrow moves in a certain pattern as shown below. Identify the pattern and choose the correct position of the block with the 3rd person.

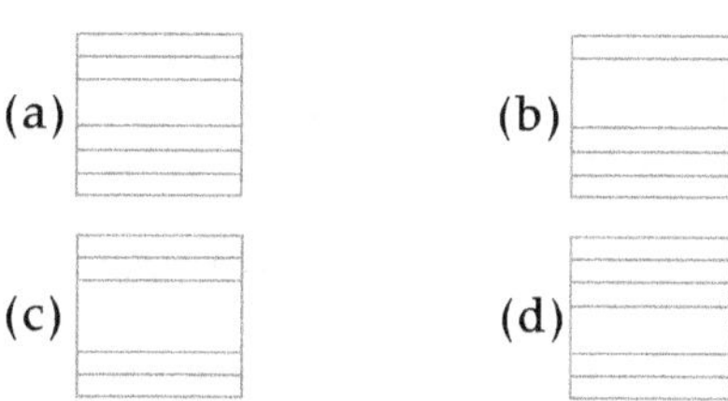

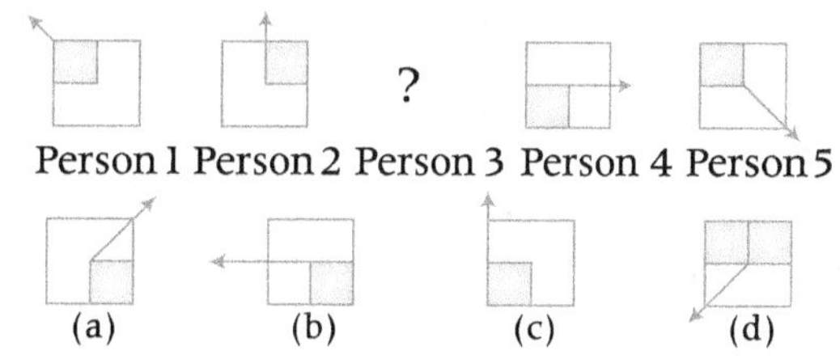

Person 1 Person 2 Person 3 Person 4 Person 5

(a)   (b)   (c)   (d)

7. In the following figures, a pattern is followed. Find the next figure which will continue the series.

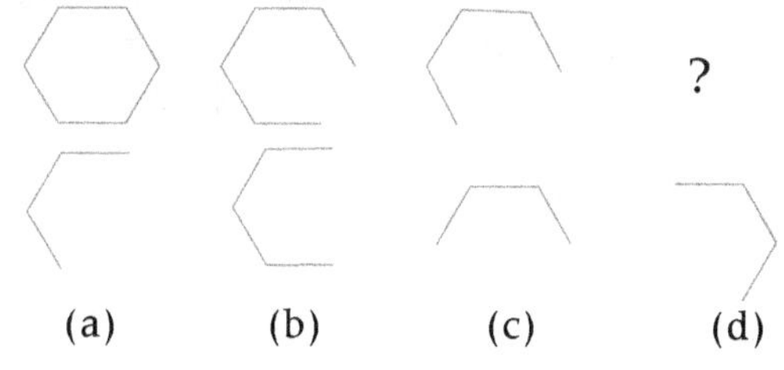

(a)   (b)   (c)   (d)

8. In a circus, certain faces were made on a tent in an order. Find the face which will continue the sequence.

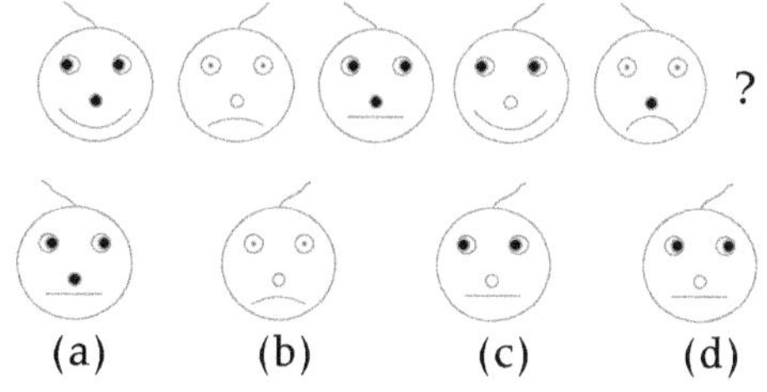

(a)   (b)   (c)   (d)

9. Observe the pattern and find the next figure.

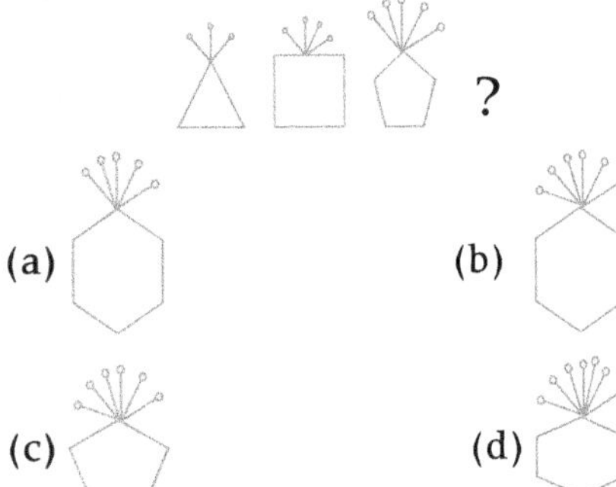

(a)   (b)

(c)   (d)

10. In the following figures, a pattern followed. Find the next figures which will continue the series?

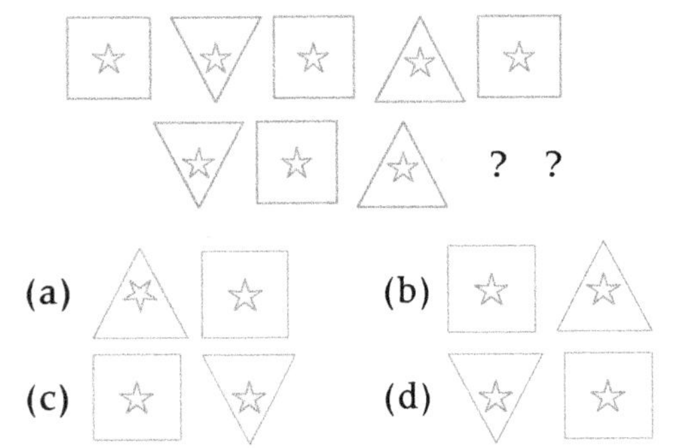

(a)   (b)

(c)   (d)

11. Given below pattern follow a certain rule. Identify the number of Boxes required in pattern in 10 by following same rule?

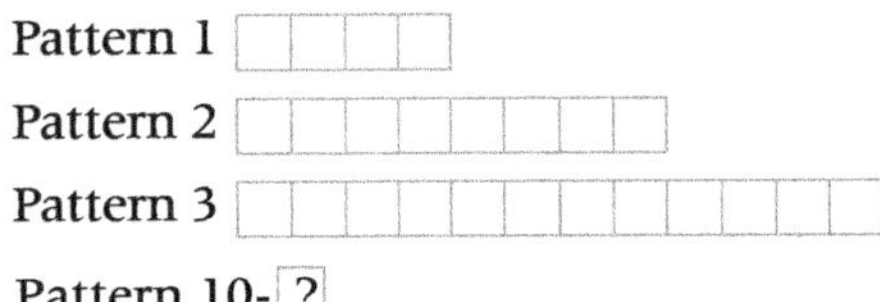

Pattern 10- ?
(a) 16 Boxes
(b) 20 Boxes
(c) 30 Boxes
(d) 40 Boxes

12. Which number will replace the question mark (?)?

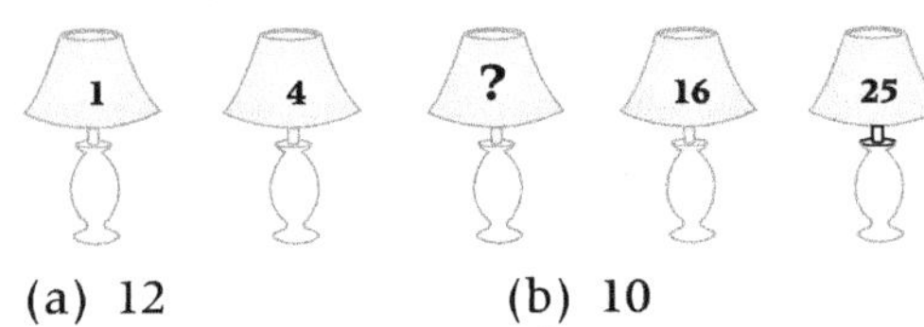

(a) 12   (b) 10
(c) 9   (d) 15

13. Find the missing card number.

(a) 13   (b) 16
(c) 12   (d) 11

14. What will be the last bag number?

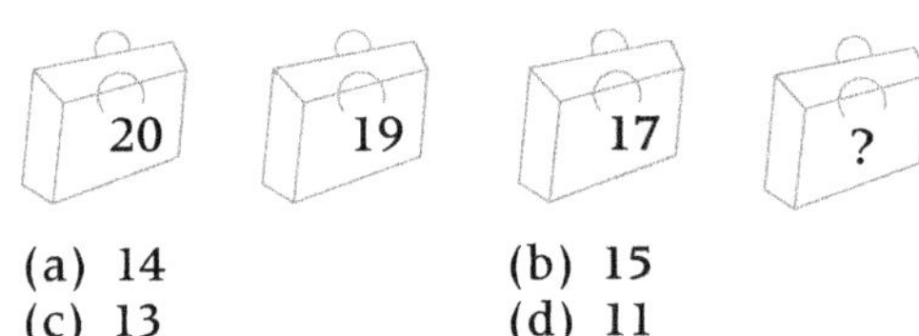

(a) 14   (b) 15
(c) 13   (d) 11

15. What number will the next t-shirt have, if they are following a certain pattern?

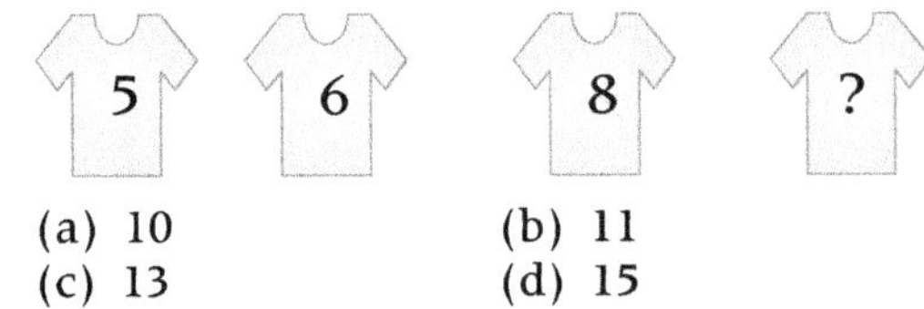

(a) 10   (b) 11
(c) 13   (d) 15

16. Bells hanging in a temple have some digits depicted on it. They are hanging in an order and the digits on the third bell is missing. Find the missing digit.

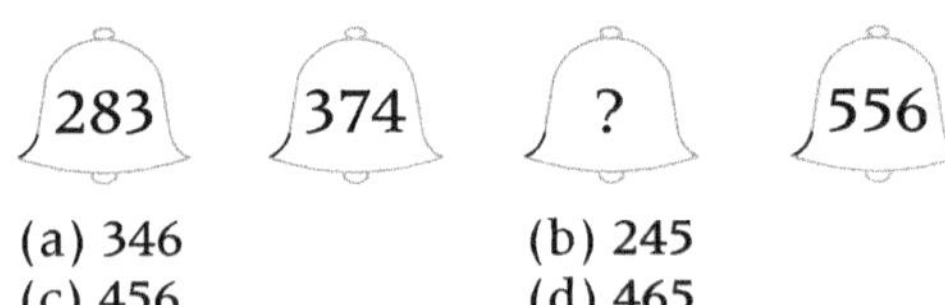

(a) 346   (b) 245
(c) 456   (d) 465

17. What number will be displayed by last LED display?

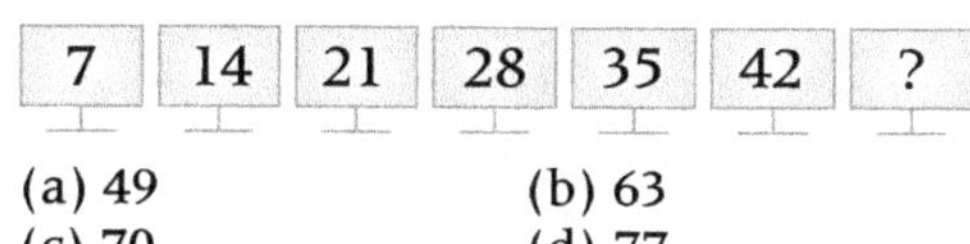

(a) 49   (b) 63
(c) 70   (d) 77

18. Which of the following numbers will come on sky 13 according to the number series shown below?

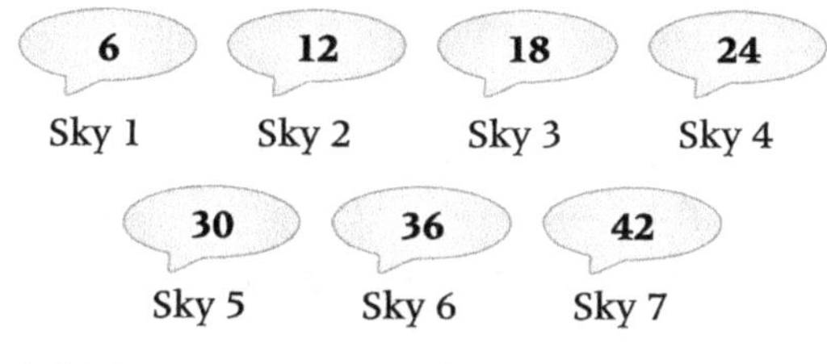

(a) 73   (b) 93
(c) 78   (d) 64

19. Ruchika used a rule to create the following pattern.

10, 14, 18, 22, 26, 30

Her friend correctly created a similar pattern using Ruchika's rule. Which pattern did Ruchika's friend create?

(a) 18, 22, 25, 29, 33, 36
(b) 16, 20, 22, 26, 31, 34
(c) 13, 17, 21, 25, 29, 33
(d) 22, 26, 30, 34, 36, 41

20. Which letter will come in last diamond?

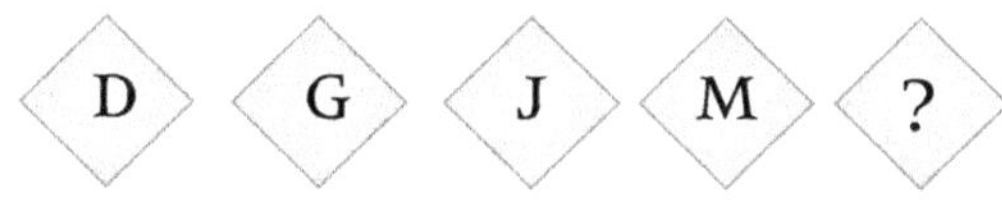

(a) P
(b) Q
(c) O
(d) T

21. The last umbrella will consists of the letters.

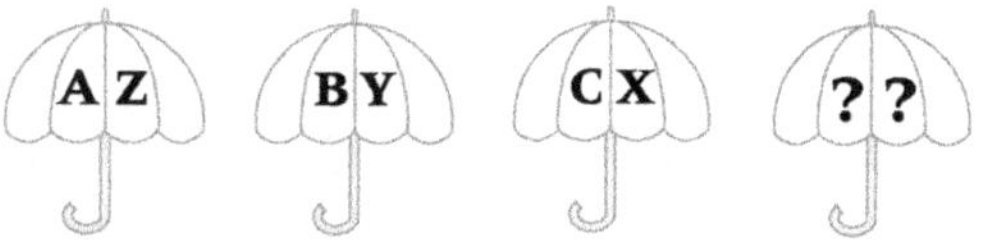

(a) DE   (b) DW   (c) XD   (d) WD

22. Which letters will continue the pattern?

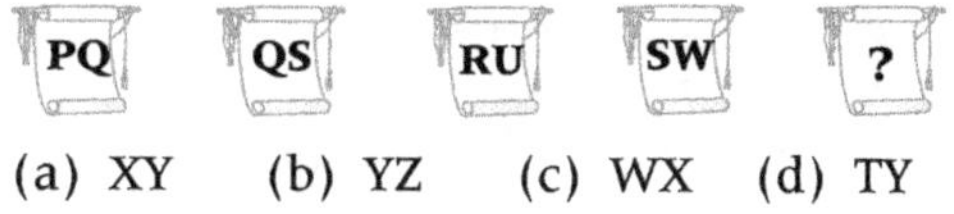

(a) XY   (b) YZ   (c) WX   (d) TY

23. In the following figures, a pattern followed. Find the next letters which will continue the series?

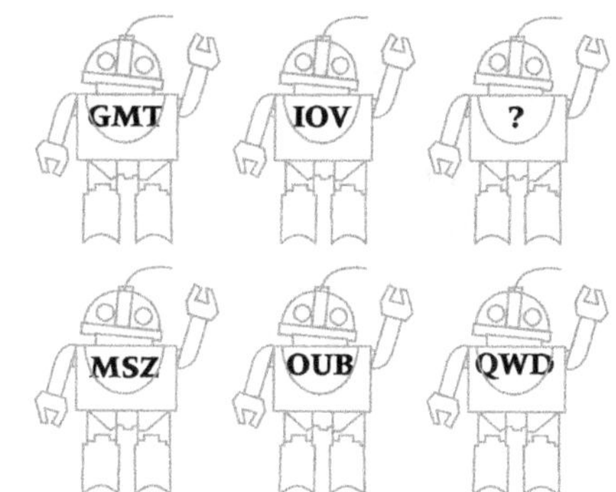

(a) KQX   (b) LSB   (c) QKW   (d) NBF

24. Which pair of letters come in last?

(a) ONK   (b) NKO   (c) KNO   (d) KON

25. Find the next letter which will continue the order?

AM   CN   EO   GP   ?

(a) IP   (b) IQ   (c) QM   (d) IT

Coding-Decoding

Coding means giving codes to the letters, numbers or shapes to hide the actual meaning. Decoding means to understand the actual meaning of the codes.

To know the concept of Coding-Decoding, let us consider the following examples

EXAMPLE 1 If 'PAPER' is coded as 'REPAP', then how will 'CURVE' be coded in the same language?

  (a) ERVCU   (b) UCREV
  (c) EVRUC   (d) REVUC

Sol. *(c)* As, 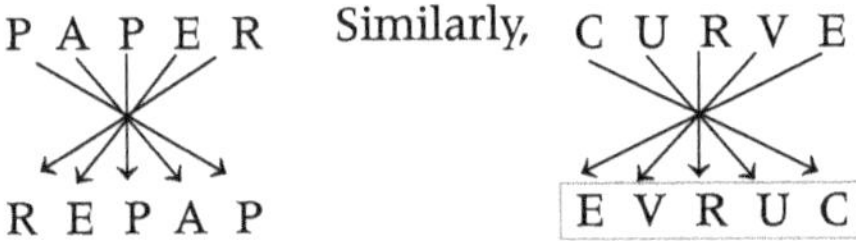

So, CURVE is coded as 'EVRUC'.

Hence, option (c) is correct.

EXAMPLE 2 In a certain code language, MANGO is coded as NBOHP, then how will the word SHAPE be coded in the same language?

  (a) TIBQF   (b) EPAHS
  (c) APESH   (d) FTIQB

Sol. *(a)* As, 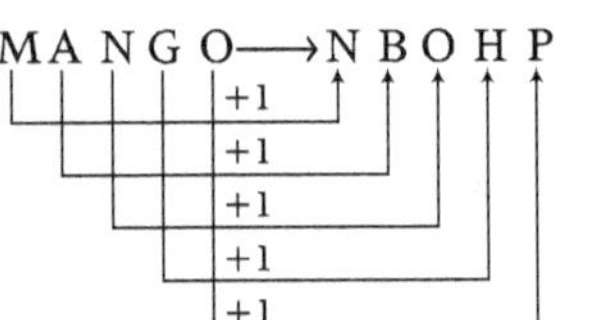 Similarly, 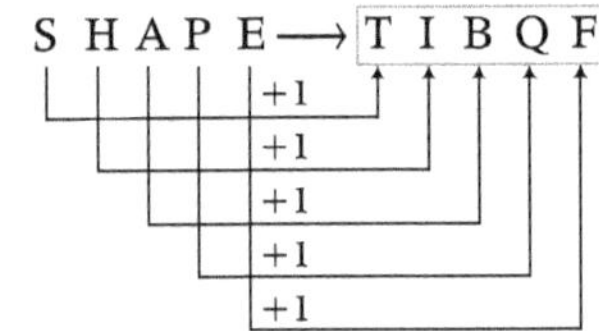

So, the code for SHAPE is 'TIBQF'.

Hence, option (a) is correct.

EXAMPLE 3   If black is called white, white is called red, red is called orange, then what is the colour of rose?

    (a) Black   (b) White

    (c) Blue   (d) Orange

Sol. *(d)* We know the colour of rose is 'red' and here red is called orange. Thus, the colour of rose is orange. Hence, option (d) is correct.

EXAMPLE 4   Study the table carefully to answer the question given below.

Letters	A	B	C	D	E	F	G	H	I	J	K	L	M	N
Codes	e	f	0	d	1	2	6	r	m	o	x	4	q	9

Find the code for 'CHAIN'.

    (a) e12rm   (b) 0rem9

    (c) xrm1d   (d) qd12m

Sol. *(b)* From the given table, the code for the word CHAIN is shown below.

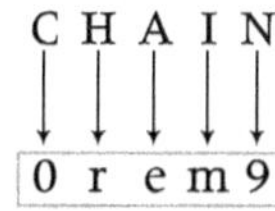

Hence, option (b) is correct.

EXAMPLE 5   If in a certain code language, A is called #, P is called @, E is called $, R is called *, then what is code for 'APPEAR'?

    (a) #@@$#*   (b) *#@@$

    (c) $#@@*   (d) #@@$*#

Sol. *(a)* As,

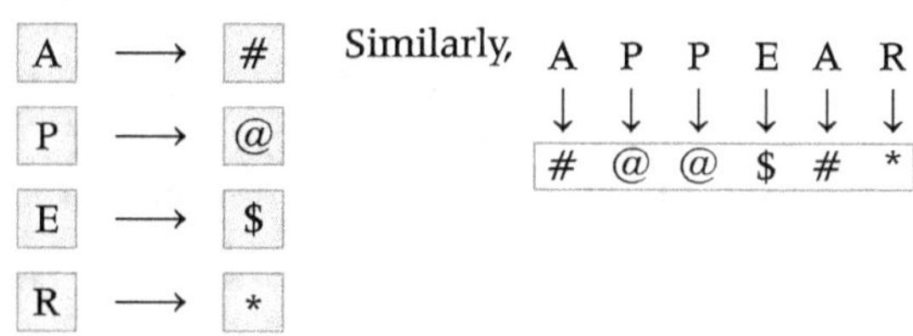

So, code for 'APPEAR' is #@@$#*.

Hence, option (a) is correct.

⏰ Let's Practice

1. If 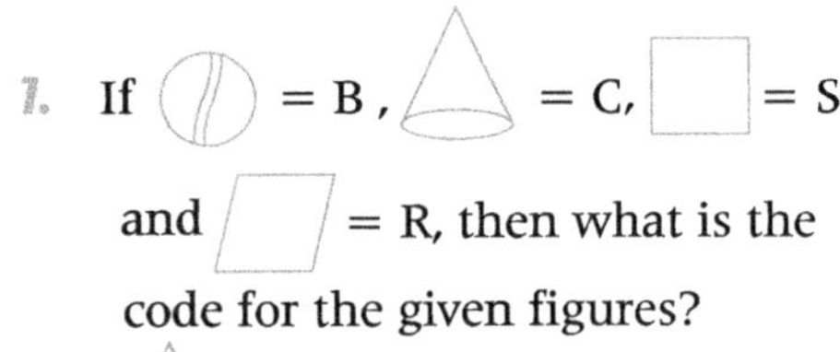 = B, = C, = S

   and = R, then what is the code for the given figures?

   (a) BCSR (b) RBCS (c) BSCR (d) CRBS

2. If 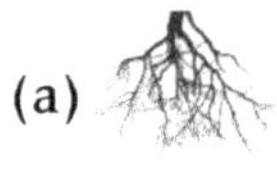 is called ,  is called 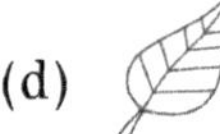 and is called .

   From which we get fruit?

   (a) (b)

   (c) (d)

3. If is coded as , is coded as and is coded as , then which shape consists of only one edge?

   (a) (b)

   (c) (d)

4. Study the table and answer the questions based on it.

Letters	A	B	C	D	E	F	G	H	I	J	K
Codes	t	x	y	i	k	n	p	r	b	e	q

   What is the code for the word 'JACK'?
   (a) ekyt   (b) nprb
   (c) etyq   (d) rtpq

5. If PAINT is coded as 74128 and EXCEL is coded as 93596, then how is ACCEPT coded?
   (a) 455978   (b) 459578
   (c) 457958   (d) 459758

6. First key is coded as CB, if its number is '32'. How will second key be coded in the same way, if its number is '54'?

   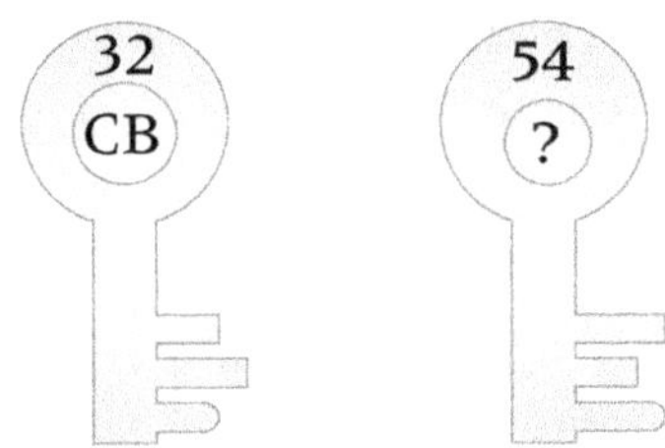

   (a) FF   (b) FE
   (c) DE   (d) ED

7. 456789 is coded for MOTHER, 7486 is the code for ?
   (a) HMET   (b) HTEM
   (c) MHET   (d) TEMH

8. In a certain code '486' means "Study very smart", 958 means "Smart work pays" which of the following is code for 'Smart'?
   (a) 4   (b) 8
   (c) 9   (d) 6

9. If 'SHOCK' is coded as HSOKC, how FROST will be coded in the same language?
   (a) RFOTS   (b) STOFR
   (c) TSORF   (d) ROSTF

10. In the figures given below the word and its code is written on the leaves of 1st figure. Following the same rule, find the code for the word in the leaf of second figure.

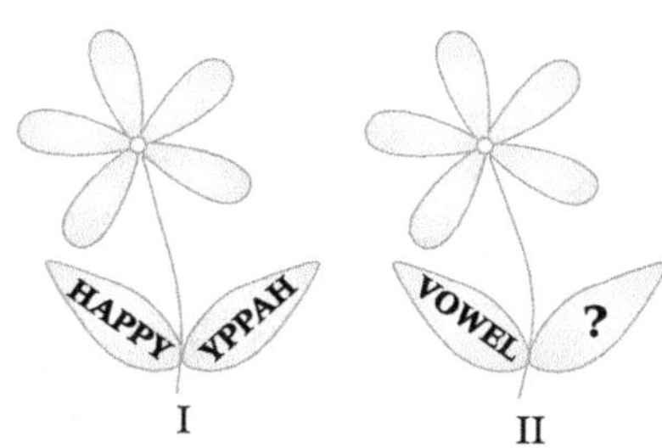

(a) ELWOY   (b) LEWOV
(c) LOVWE   (d) ELWVO

11. If PLANET is coded as QMBOFU, then how BETTER will be coded in the same language?
(a) RETEBE   (b) DFTURE
(c) CFUUFS   (d) ETTERB

12. If SNAKE is coded as UPCMG, then what will be the code for JAPAN?
(a) NAPAJ   (b) LCRCP
(c) APJAN   (d) AJPNA

13. If in a certain code language, RAT is written as '*Δ%' and 'CAT' is written as '# Δ%', then how will CAR be written in that language?
(a) $%Δ   (b) #%Δ
(c) #Δ*   (d) Δ*%

14. If in a certain code language, S is written as '5', 'N' is written as '@', 'O' is written as 'g', 'W' is written as '#'.
Then, how we write SNOW in coded language?
(a) @5g#   (b) 5@g#
(c) #g@5   (d) 5@#g

15. COOK is coded as @<<#, MOCK is coded as %<@#, How is COCK coded?
(a) @%<<   (b) @<##
(c) @<%#   (d) @<@#

16. If 'butter' is called 'soap', 'soap' is called 'ink', 'ink' is called 'honey', then which of the following is used for washing clothes?
(a) Orange   (b) Butter
(c) Ink   (d) Honey

17. If 'finger' is called 'nose', 'nose' is called 'tongue' and 'tongue' is called 'foot', then with which organ does a man tastes food?
(a) Foot   (b) Hand
(c) Finger   (d) Nose

18. If Lucknow is called Patna, Patna is called Kolkata, Kolkata is called Gandhinagar. Then, what is the capital of West Bengal?
(a) Lucknow
(b) Patna
(c) Gandhinagar
(d) Kolkata

19. If ₹ is called ¥, ¥ is called £ and £ is called $, then what is the symbol of currency of India?
(a) ₹   (b) ¥
(c) £   (d) $

20. If III means IV, IV means V, V means VI and VI means VII, then which comes immediately after IV in counting?
(a) V   (b) III
(c) VII   (d) VI

21. If V means X, X means C, C means XII, then which comes immediately after IX in counting?
(a) VI   (b) C   (c) X   (d) XII

22. The following question is based on the coded instructions given in the table.

Code	Instructions
1	Put two MANGOES in a basket
2	Put two Dairy Milk in a basket
3	Take out 1 Mango in a basket
4	Take out 1 Dairy milk in a basket
5	Put 2 Ice-creams in a basket

observe this :
How many items would be in a basket if you are ordered for code 123?
(a) 3   (b) 4
(c) 5   (d) 6

Chapter 05

Alphabet and Word Formation Test

Alphabet Test

In Alphabet test, we will deal with different topics which are as follow

- Inserting a letter to form two meaningful words.
- Arrangement of letters to form a meaningful word and determining its category.
- Finding a word which can or cannot be formed using the letters of the given word.
- Number of letters skipped in between adjacent letters.

In 'alphabet test', following types of questions are generally asked.

EXAMPLE 1 Which letter from the given alternatives will replace the question mark (?) and form two meaningful words?

	P		
R	?	A	R
	R		
	E		

 (a) E   (b) O   (c) T   (d) D

Sol. *(b)* The letter 'O' will replace the question mark(?) and form two meaningful words, i.e. PORE and ROAR. Hence, option (b) is correct.

EXAMPLE 2 Find the correct combination of numbers, so that when letters are arranged accordingly, form a meaningful word.

$$\begin{array}{ccccc} A & I & M & C & G \\ 1 & 2 & 3 & 4 & 5 \end{array}$$

 (a) 53214   (b) 41325   (c) 31524   (d) 21354

Sol. *(c)* Word which can be formed using the given letters is MAGIC.
So, the arrangement of numbers is '31524'.
Hence, option (c) is correct.

EXAMPLE 3   Find the word which can be formed using the letters of the given word.

REPEAT

    (a) TREAT   (b) PEAR

    (c) PINE   (d) NEAT

Sol. *(b)* The word PEAR can be formed using the letters of the given word since all the letters of the word PEAR are present in the given word. Hence, option (b) is correct.

EXAMPLE 4   Find the category of given word so formed when the letters are arranged in a meaningful manner.

ASDYI

    (a) Cloth   (b) Fruit

    (c) Flower   (d) Vegetable

Sol. *(c)* The word formed will be DAISY from the given letters and DAISY is a flower. Hence, option (c) is correct.

Word Formation Test

Word Formation or Logical arrangement of words means arranging the given words according to the dictionary or in a meaningful order. To answer this type of questions, one must know the sequence of letters and meanings of words.

In logical arrangement of words, following types of questions are generally asked.

EXAMPLE 5   Arrange the given words as they occur in the dictionary.

    1. Candle   2. Paper   3. Mango   4. Doctor

    (a) 4132   (b) 1432

    (c) 3241   (d) 2314

Sol. *(b)* The given words can be arranged in the dictionary considering their first letter starting from A, B, ..., Z.

Now, the given words can be arranged with the first word 'Candle', (starting letter 'C'), then 'Doctor', (starting letter 'D'), then 'Mango' and then 'Paper'. So, the correct sequence is '1432'. Hence, option (b) is correct.

EXAMPLE 6   Arrange the given words in meaningful order.

    1. Plant   2. Tree   3. Seed   4. Wood

    (a) 3124   (b) 4132

    (c) 2341   (d) 1342

Sol. *(a)* The logical arrangement of words in meaningful order is as follows:

Seed → Plant → Tree → Wood
3   1   2   4

So, the sequence is '3124'.

Hence, option (a) is correct.

⏰ Let's Practice

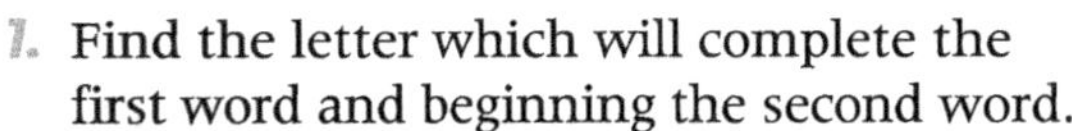

1. Find the letter which will complete the first word and beginning the second word.

    B I R ⟨?⟩ U C K

    (a) T   (b) K
    (c) L   (d) D

2. Which letter from the given alternatives will replace the question mark(?) and form two meaningful words?

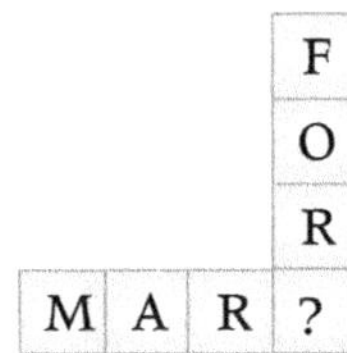

    (a) A   (b) T
    (c) L   (d) S

3. Find the letter which will complete the first word and beginning the second word.

    S H A P (?) Y E S

    (a) E   (b) K
    (c) N   (d) O

4. Which letter should be replaced with the question mark (?) to form two meaningful words?

    (a) B   (b) A   (c) T   (d) D

5. Choose the category of the given word so formed when the letters are arranged meaningfully.

    ADHN

    (a) Body part   (b) Cloth
    (c) Fruit   (d) Flower

6. Choose the correct combination of numbers so that letters arranged accordingly form a meaningful word.

    H S R I T
    1 2 3 4 5

    (a) 21435   (b) 54132
    (c) 32415   (d)13542

7. Choose the word which can be formed using the letters of the given word.

    EXERCISE

    (a) RAISE   (b) RISE
    (c) SEAT   (d) TEAR

8. Select from the given alternatives the word which cannot be formed using the letters of the given word.

    EDUCATION

    (a) NEAT   (b) ACTION
    (c) DEAN   (d) NATION

9. Which letter occurs once in word REPEAT, and ARTIST but not at all in word REPEL?

    (a) P   (b) R
    (c) E   (d) A

Directions (Q. Nos. 10 and 11) Answer the following questions based on the sequence of letters given below.

U E I L C F P A K M B G D O H Q J R N S V X Z T Y W

10. Which of the following letter is 3rd from the left?

    (a) L   (b) I
    (c) T   (d) F

11. If we dropped all the vowels then which of the following letter is 2nd from the right end?

    (a) C   (b) Z
    (c) Y   (d) P

12. Arrange the following words according to English dictionary.

    1. Bunch   2. Petition
    3. Improve   4. Direct
    (a) 4132   (b) 3241
    (c) 1432   (d) 2341

13. Which one of the given responses is the correct order of words as per dictionary?

    1. Host   2. Resident
    3. Harmony   4. Raise
    (a) 3142   (b) 2143
    (c) 1342   (d) 4132

14. Arrange the following words in meaningful order.

    1. Week   2. Year
    3. Month   4. Day
    (a) 3142   (b) 2341
    (c) 1432   (d) 4132

15. Which one will be the correct sequence of the given words in meaningful order?

    1. Frog   2. Grass
    3. Snake   4. Grasshopper
    (a) 1432   (b) 3421
    (c) 2413   (d) 4321

16. Arrange the given words in alphabetical order.

    1. House   2. Elephant
    3. Tiger   4. Lion

    (a) 1, 2, 3, 4   (b) 2, 1, 4, 3
    (c) 3, 4, 1, 2   (d) 4, 3, 2, 1

17. Arrange the following words in the meaningful order?

    1. Chin   2. Head
    3. Nose   4. Legs
    (a) 4, 3, 1, 2   (b) 2, 3, 1, 4
    (c) 4, 2, 3, 1   (d) 1, 2, 4, 3

18. Only one number is skipped in between adjacent letters. Which of the following group of letters is following the above rule?

    (a) A B D G   (b) L N O Q
    (c) L N O R   (d) B E G H

Directions (Q. Nos. 19 and 20) In each of the following questions, find the two words, one from each group that together make a new meaningful word. The word from the first group always came first.

19.

1	2	3
Cloth	Corona	Mug

A	B	C
tion	Paper	Virus

    (a) 1B   (b) 3A
    (c) 2C   (d) 2B

20.

1	2	3
Video	Water	Milk

X	Y	Z
Sheet	Game	Air

    (a) 1Z   (b) 2X
    (c) 3Z   (d) 1Y

Complete the Figure

Pattern completion means finding out the missing figure in a given set of figures following a certain rule. To understand how we complete the given set of figures, have a look on the following example.

EXAMPLE 1 Anny drew a pattern on a cardboard as shown below. Complete the pattern from the given alternatives.

Sol. *(d)* The figure in option (d) will complete the pattern. The completed pattern can be shown as

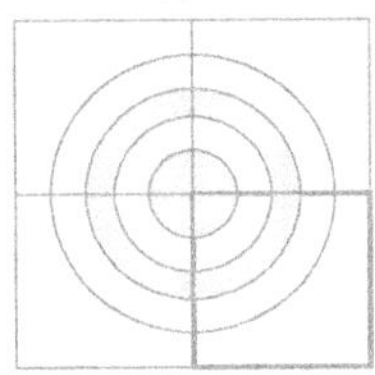

Hence, option (d) is correct.

EXAMPLE 2 Complete the missing pattern of the block.

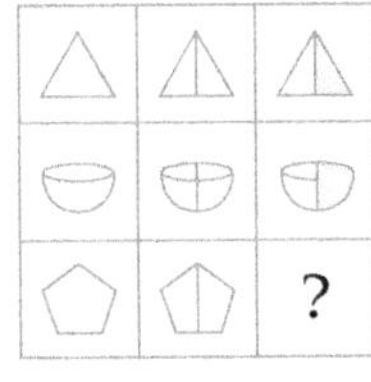

Sol. *(d)* In all the rows, first element is divided into two equal parts to get the second element and then its right half part gets shaded in the third column.

So, the last element of the third row will be the element in option (d).

Hence, option (d) is correct.

⏰ Let's Practice

1. What will be the pattern made on the fourth tile?

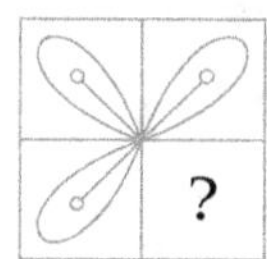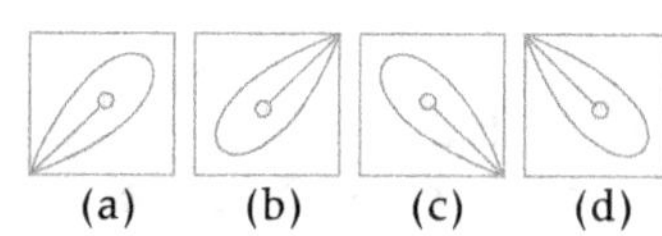

   (a)   (b)   (c)   (d)

2. Find the figure which will complete the given pattern.

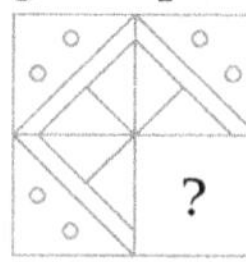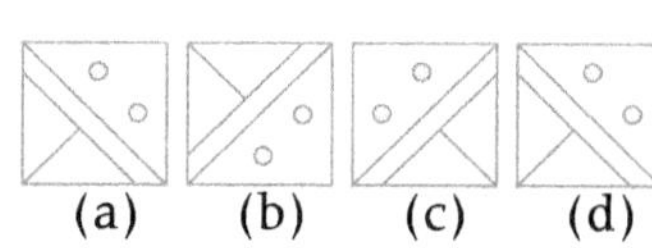

   (a)   (b)   (c)   (d)

3. Mixi drew the following rangoli pattern in her drawing notebook. Complete the pattern.

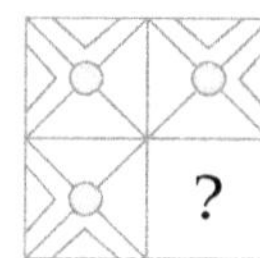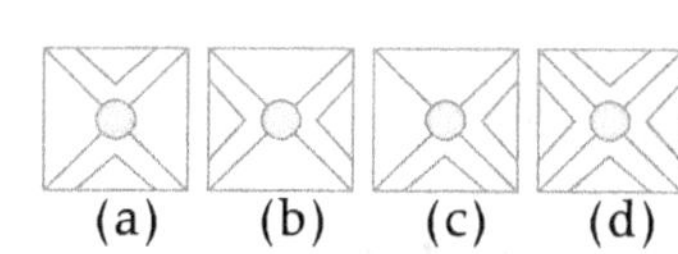

   (a)   (b)   (c)   (d)

4. Mani drew the following pattern and asked her friend to complete the pattern. Which figure will complete the pattern?

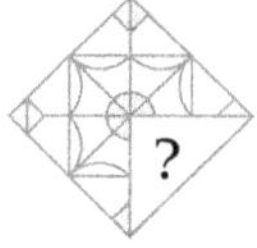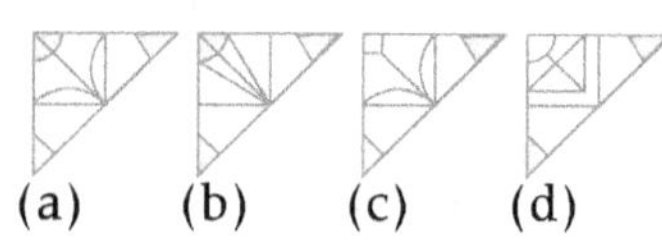

   (a)   (b)   (c)   (d)

5. Complete the pattern of the spider web.

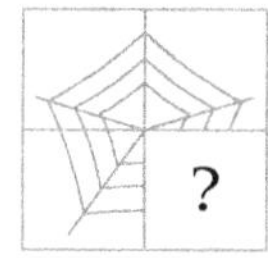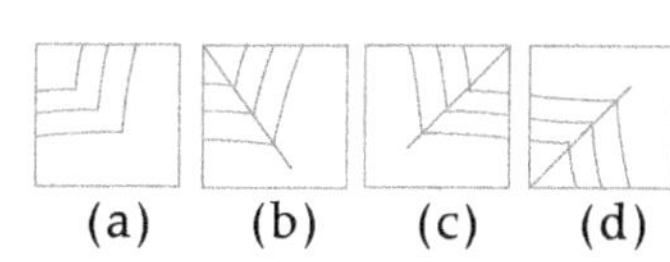

   (a)   (b)   (c)   (d)

6. The missing pattern of the Harper's book cover will be

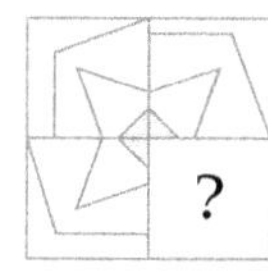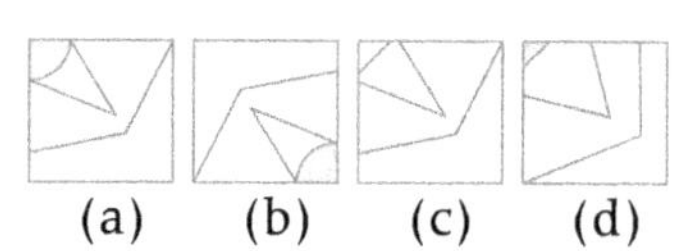

   (a)   (b)   (c)   (d)

7. Complete the pattern in the given box.

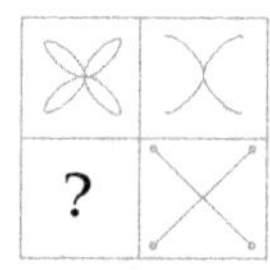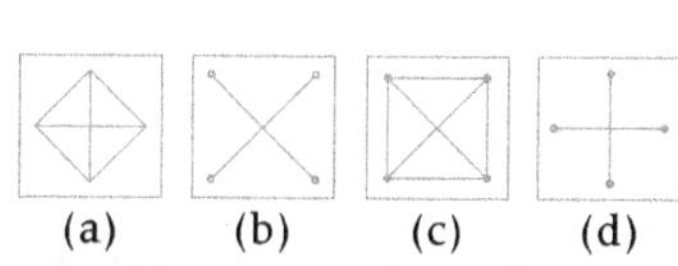

   (a)   (b)   (c)   (d)

8. Select a suitable figure from the four alternatives that would complete the figure matrix.

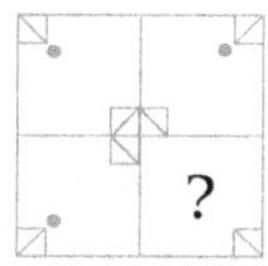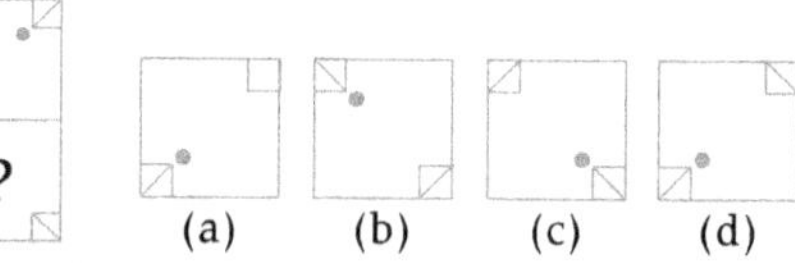

   (a)   (b)   (c)   (d)

9. Find the figure which will complete the given pattern.

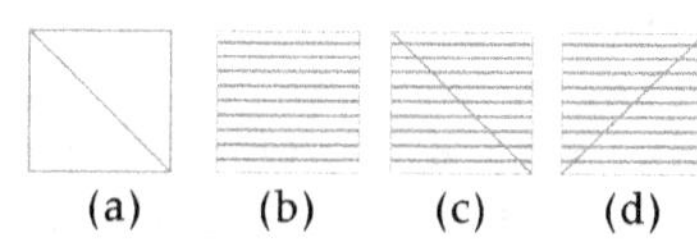

   (a)   (b)   (c)   (d)

10. Find the figure which will complete the given pattern.

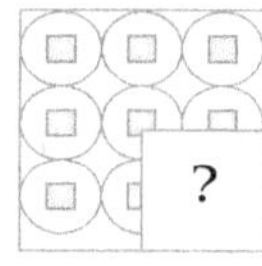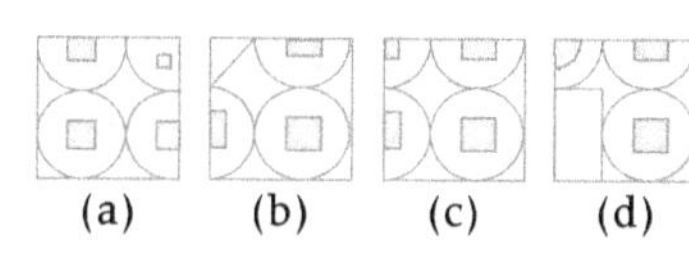

   (a)   (b)   (c)   (d)

11. Find the figure which will complete the given pattern.

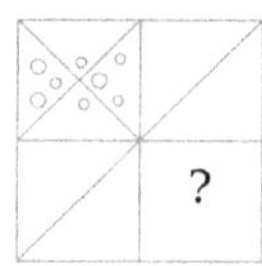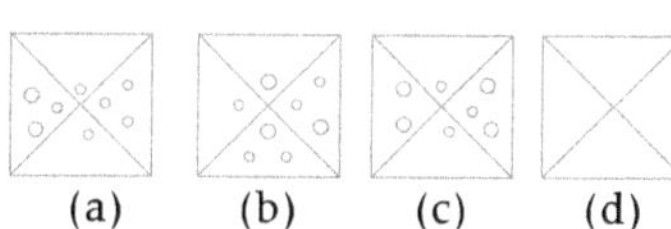

   (a)   (b)   (c)   (d)

12. Find the figure which will complete the given pattern.

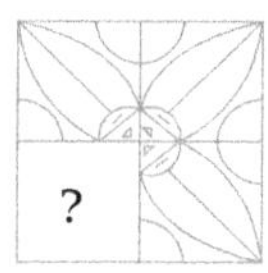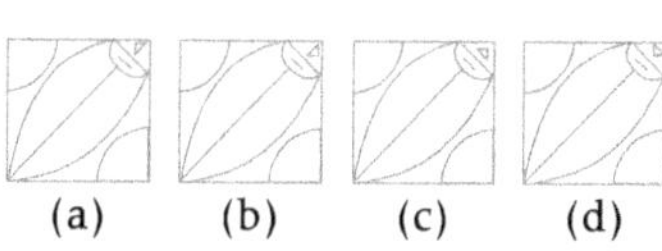

   (a)   (b)   (c)   (d)

13. Dake saw the four tiles and remember only the pattern of three tiles. Find the pattern of the fourth tile.

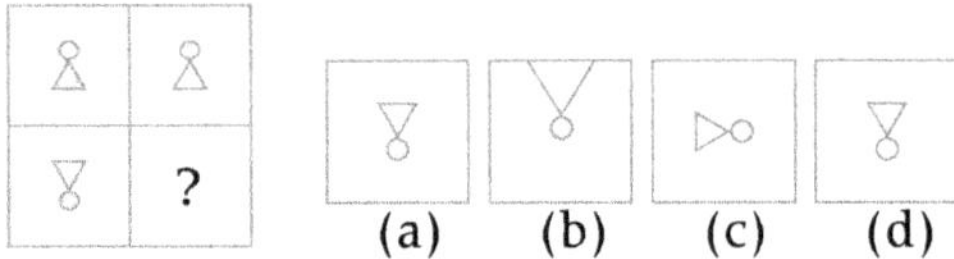

14. Find the figure which will complete the given pattern?

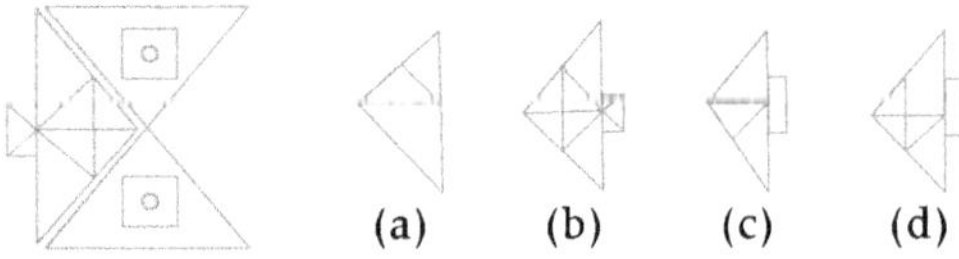

15. Complete the pattern in the given matrix.

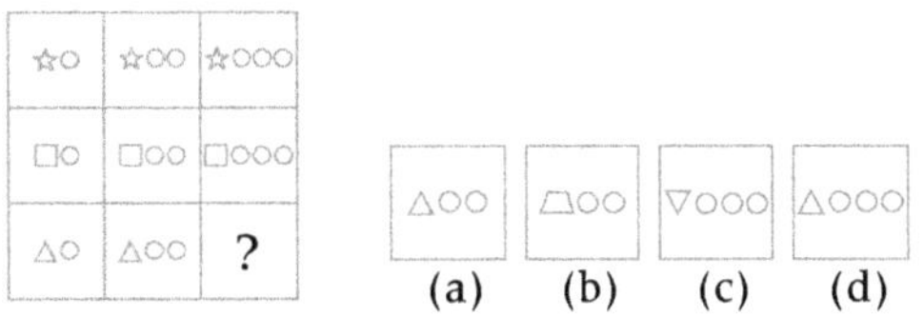

16. Pixie drew following patterns. What will be the pattern in the last block?

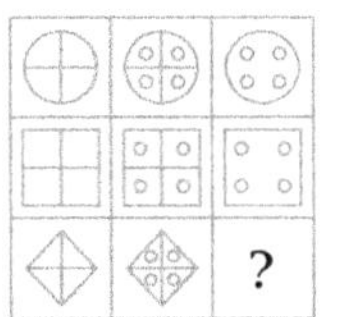 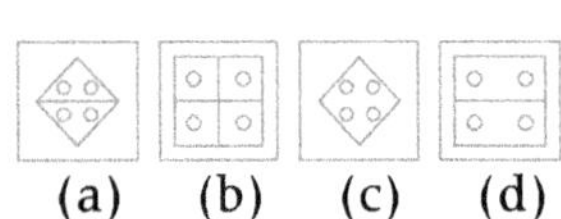

17. Complete the pattern of the tiles on the wall.

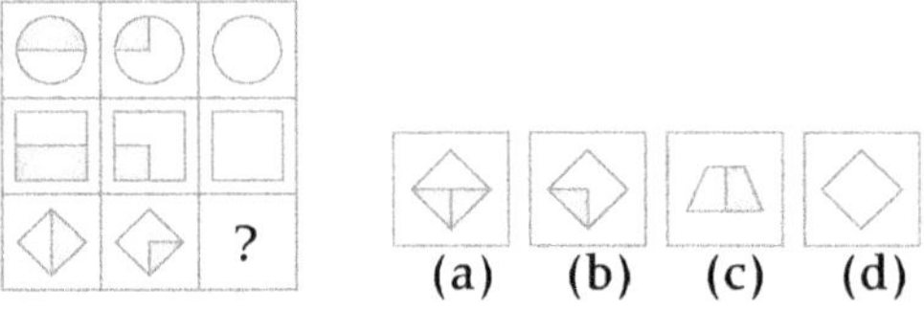

18. Jack drew following patterns. What will be come at the place of question mark(?)?

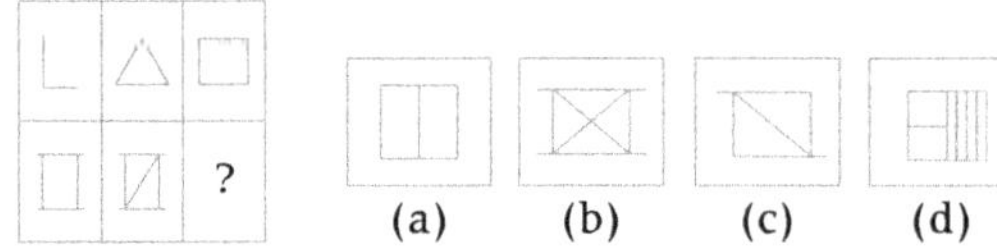

19. Complete the pattern in the given matrix?

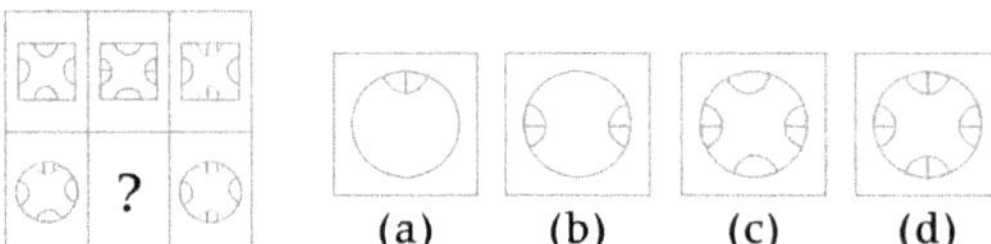

20. Select a suitable figure from the four alternative that would complete the figure matrix.

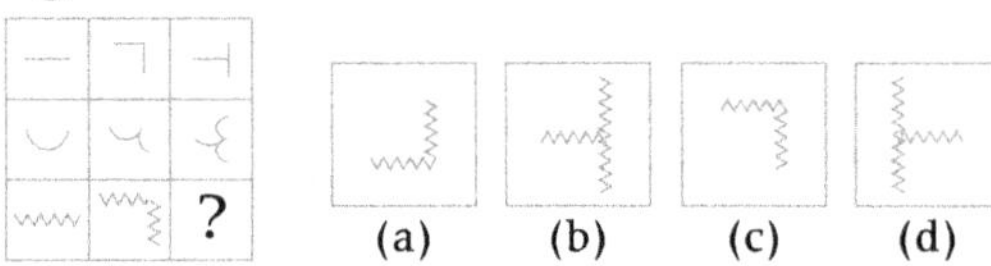

Hidden Figures

A figure is said to be hidden in another figure, if that figure is embedded or completely in another figure as its part.

To understand the concept of hidden figure, let's have a look on the following example.

EXAMPLE 1 Anny observed the four different keys of locks and asked his brother to find out the key in which given zig-zag form (X) is hidden?

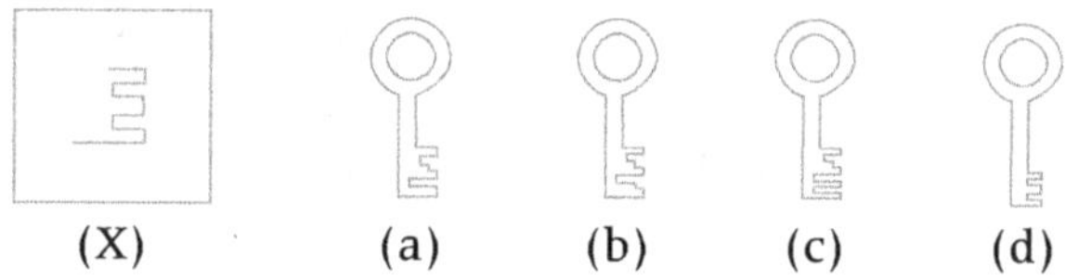

Sol. *(d)* The given zig-zag form is hidden in the key given in option (d), i.e.

Hence, option (d) is correct.

EXAMPLE 2   Some shapes were drawn on a piece of paper, then find which of the following shape is hidden in the figure (X) given below?

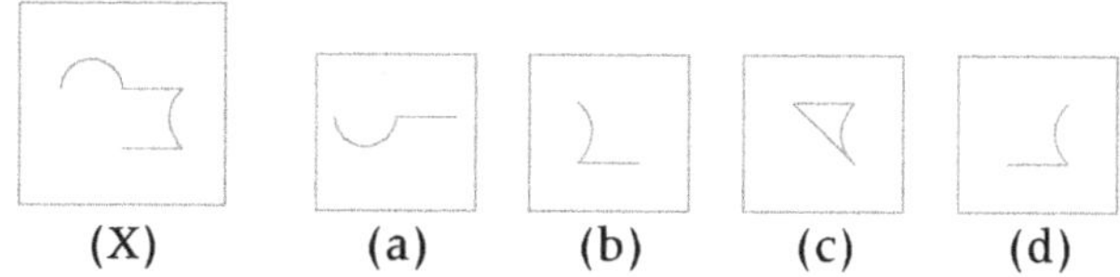

Sol. *(d)* Option figure (d) is hidden in the main figure which is as shown in adjacent figure.

Hence, option (d) is correct.

⏰ Let's Practice

1. Find the the figure from the alternatives which is correctly embedded in the problem figure (X).

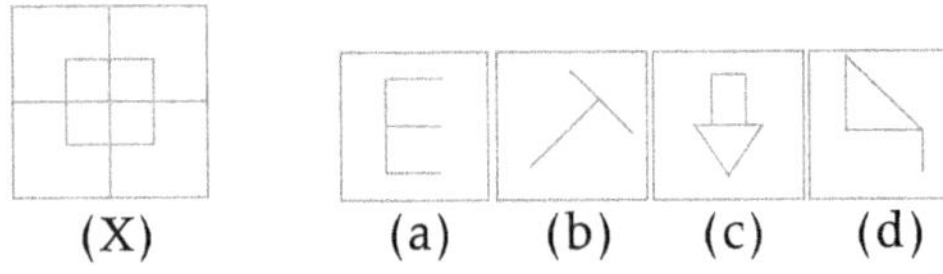

(X)   (a)   (b)   (c)   (d)

2. Which of the following figure from the alternatives is exactly hidden in the problem figure (X)?

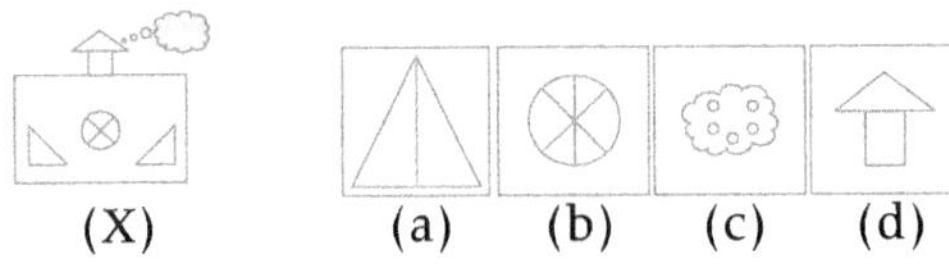

(X)   (a)   (b)   (c)   (d)

3. Which of the following figure from the alternatives is exactly embedded in the given figure (X)?

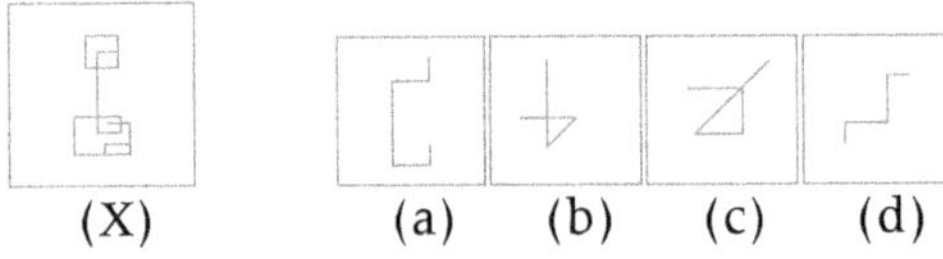

(X)   (a)   (b)   (c)   (d)

4. Which of the following shape is exactly embedded in the problem figure (X)?

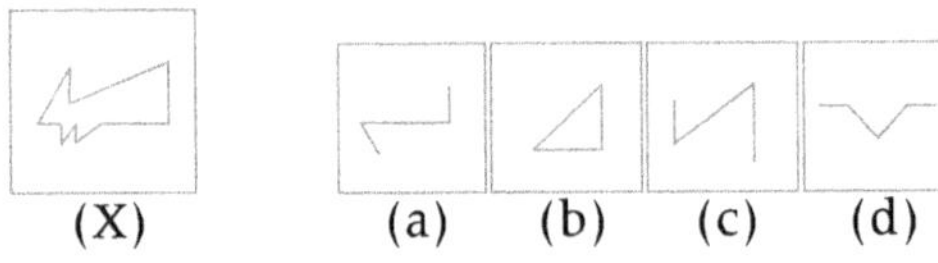

(X)   (a)   (b)   (c)   (d)

5. Identify the figure from the alternatives which is exactly hidden in the problem figure (X).

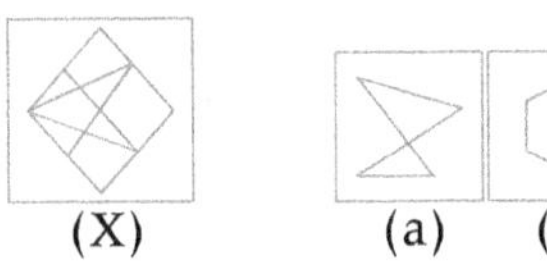 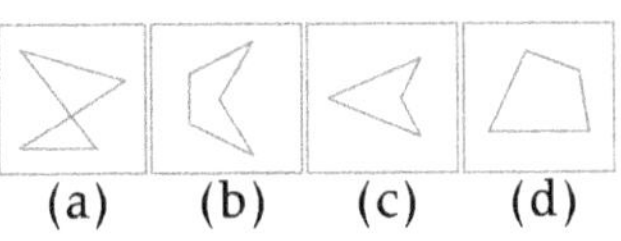

(X)   (a)   (b)   (c)   (d)

6. Identify the figure which is exactly embedded in the given figure (X).

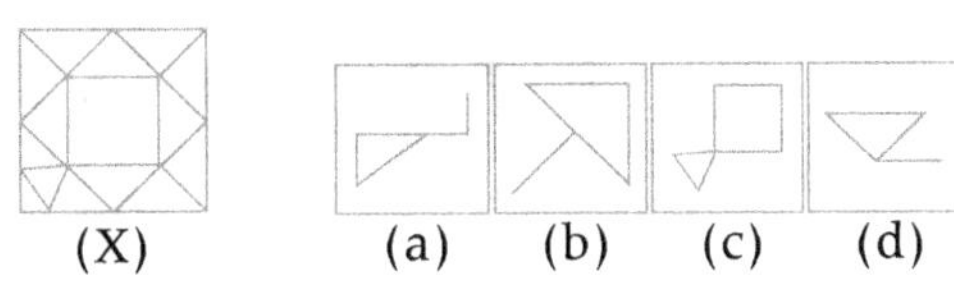

(X)   (a)   (b)   (c)   (d)

7. Find the figure from the alternatives which is exactly hidden in the problem figure (X).

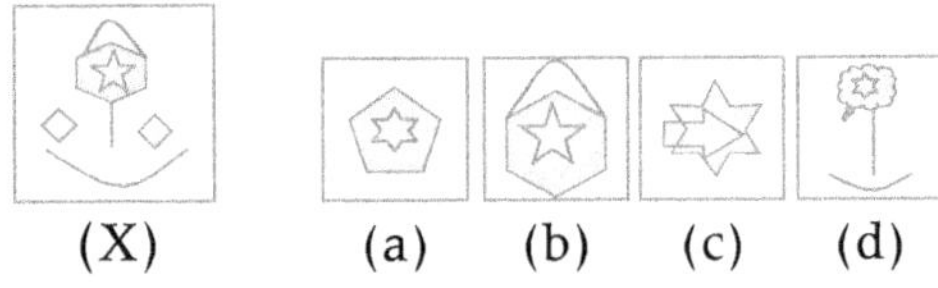

(X)   (a)   (b)   (c)   (d)

8. Identify the part of the figure which is not embedded in the question figure.

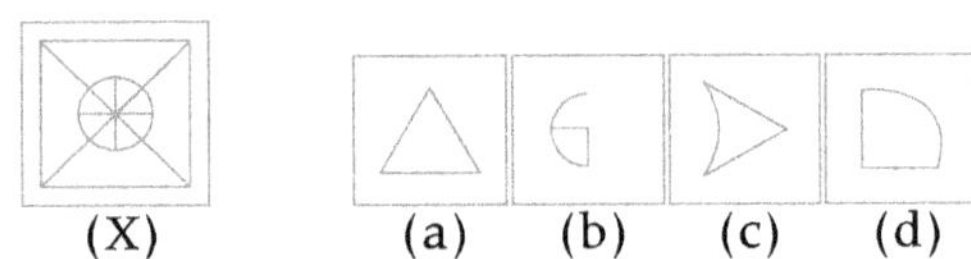

(X)   (a)   (b)   (c)   (d)

9. Find the part of the figure which is not hidden in the problem figure (X).

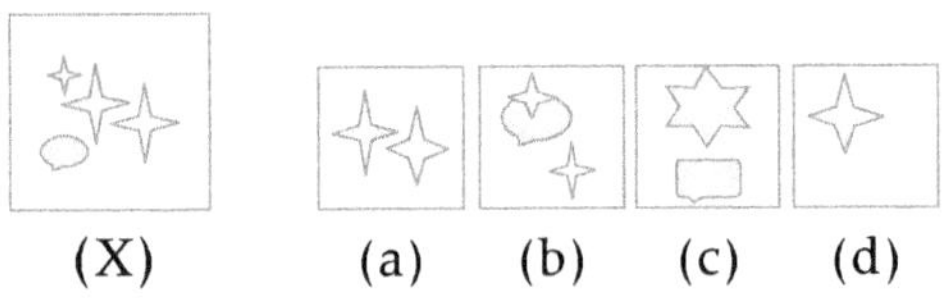

(X)   (a)   (b)   (c)   (d)

10. Find the part of the figure which is not hidden in the problem figure (X).

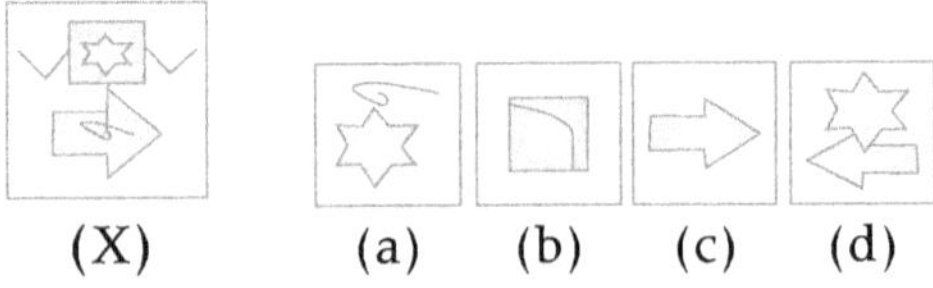

(X)   (a)   (b)   (c)   (d)

11. A teacher drew some shapes on the board and asked the students to find the figure in which figure (X) is hidden.

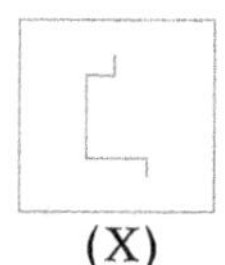 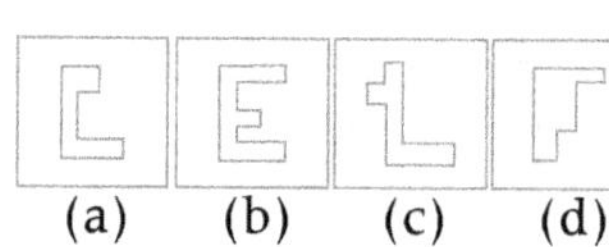

(X)   (a)   (b)   (c)   (d)

12. In which of the following figures, the given figure (X) is embedded?

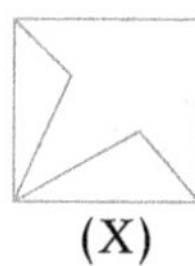 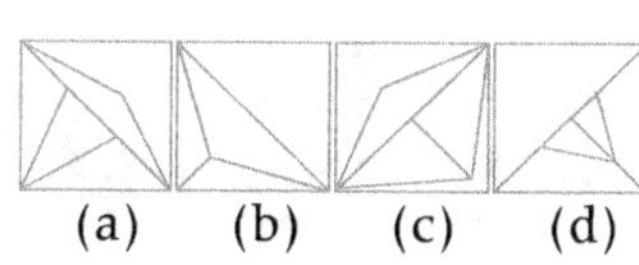

(X)   (a)   (b)   (c)   (d)

13. Find the figure in which the given figure (X) is exactly embedded.

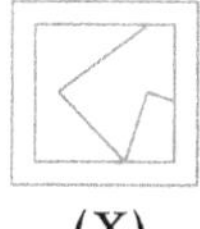 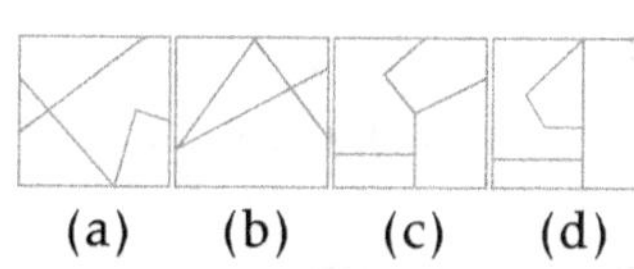

(X)   (a)   (b)   (c)   (d)

14. In which of the following figure the given figure (X) is embedded?

 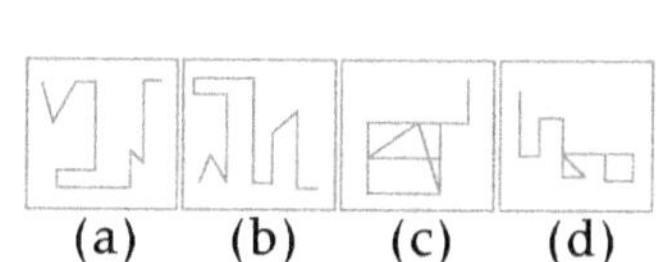

(X)   (a)   (b)   (c)   (d)

15. Identify the figure in which the problem figure (X) is hidden.

 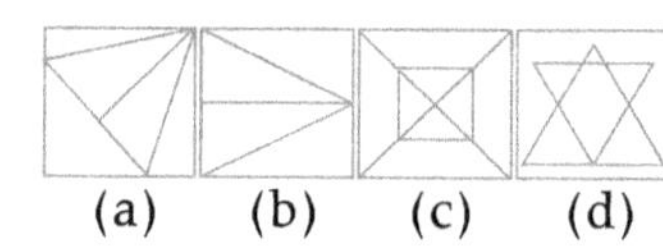

(X)   (a)   (b)   (c)   (d)

16. In which of the following figures the given figure (X) is embedded?

 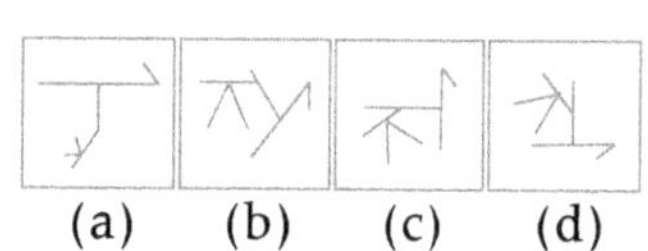

(X)   (a)   (b)   (c)   (d)

17. The given shape (X) is used to make one of the following designs. Which design contains the given shape (X)?

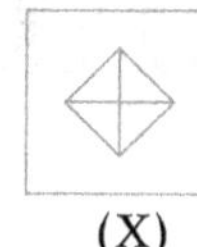 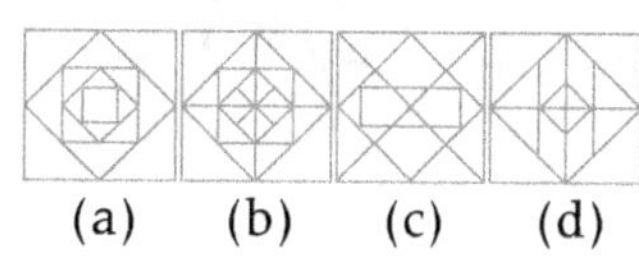

(X)   (a)   (b)   (c)   (d)

18. Identify the figure in which the problem figure (X) is hidden.

 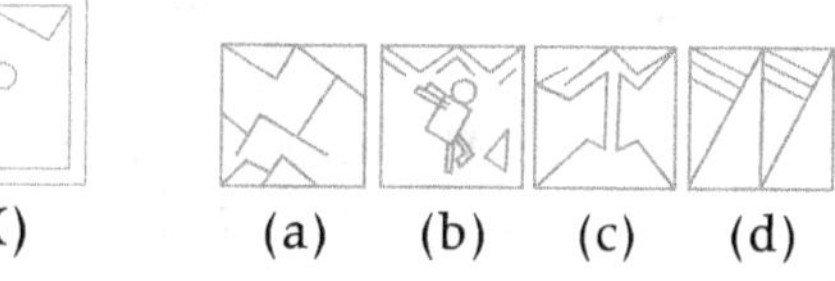

(X)   (a)   (b)   (c)   (d)

19. Identify the figure in which the problem figure (X) is hidden.

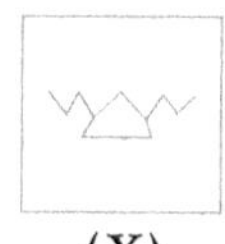 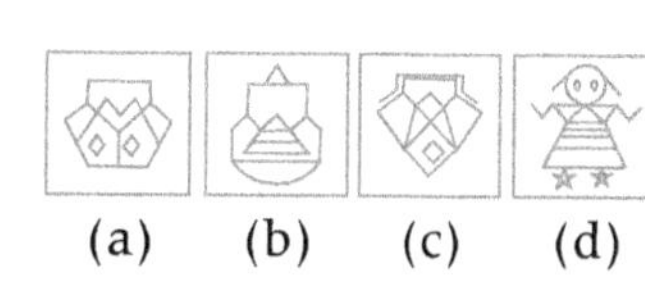

(X)   (a)   (b)   (c)   (d)

20. Identify the figure in which the problem figure (X) is hidden.

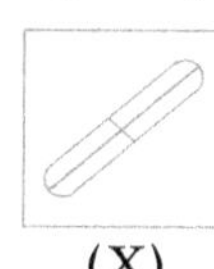 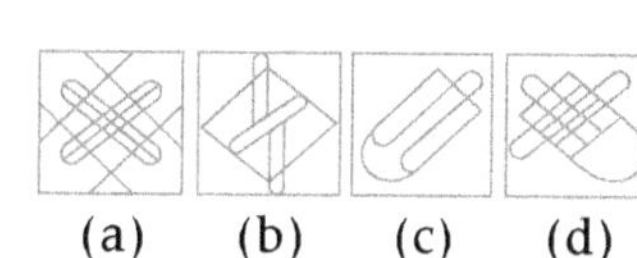

(X)   (a)   (b)   (c)   (d)

Counting of Figures

In counting of figures, we count different geometrical shapes like lines, triangles, circles, rectangles, squares, etc., from a given complex figure.

Let's have a look on the following examples to understand the concept of this chapter.

EXAMPLE 1 Michael drew a figure consisting of many rectangles and asked his friend to count the number of rectangles from it. How many rectangles are there in the given figure?

(a) 8   (b) 7   (c) 6   (d) 10

Sol. *(a)* To count the number of rectangles first we label the figure as shown in adjacent figure.

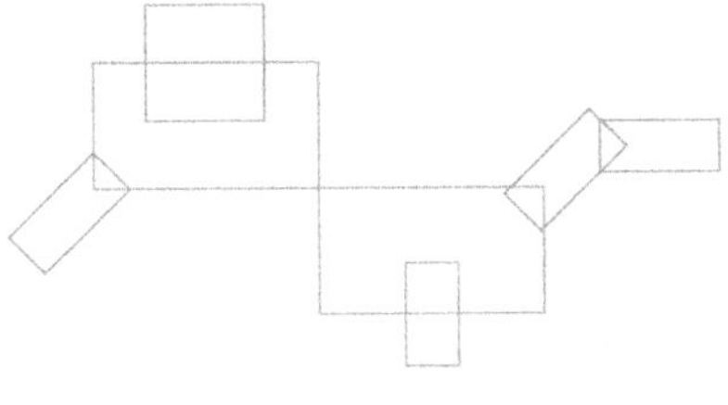

So, there are eight rectangles when they are counted.

Hence, option (a) is correct.

EXAMPLE 2 Count the number of lines in the given figure.

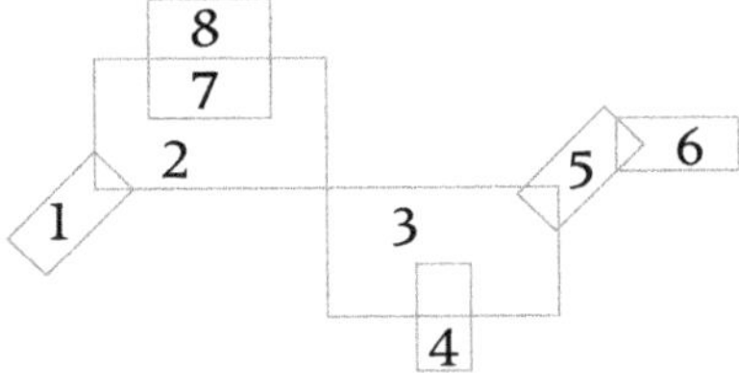

(a) 13   (b) 8   (c) 10   (d) 14

Sol. (b) 

Horizontal line ⎯ = 4
Vertical lines ╱ = 4
Total number of lines are = 4 + 4 = 8

EXAMPLE 3   Count the number of triangles in the following figure.

   (a) 6   (b) 8
   (c) 10   (d) 9

Sol. (d) To count the number of triangles in the given figure, first we
label it as shown in figure given below. The smaller triangles are 5.
Triangles made up of two small triangles are = 4
∴ Total number of triangles = 5 + 4 = 9
Hence, option (d) is correct.

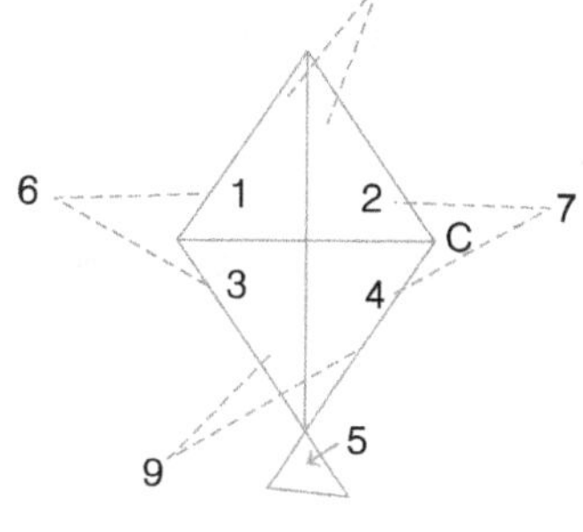

EXAMPLE 4   How many squares are there in the following figure?

   (a) 6   (b) 5   (c) 4   (d) 8

Sol. (b) The given figure can be labelled as shown in adjoining figure.
Number of smaller squares = 4
Largest square = 1
∴ Total number of squares = 4 + 1 = 5
Hence, option (b) is correct.

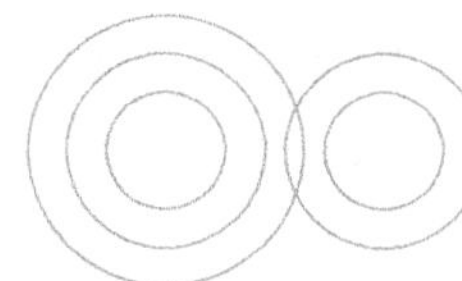

EXAMPLE 5   Find out the number of circles in the given figure.

   (a) 4   (b) 6   (c) 5   (d) 8

Sol. (c) The given circles can be labelled as shown in adjoining figure.
Total number of circles is 5 when they are counted.
Hence, option (c) is correct.

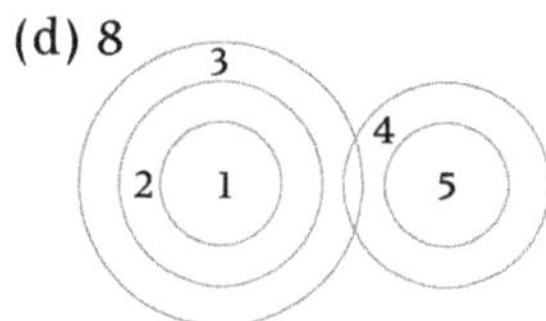

⏰ Let's Practice

1. Find out the number of rectangles in the given figure.

   (a) 9   (b) 13
   (c) 10   (d) 11

2. Count the number of lines in the figure given below.

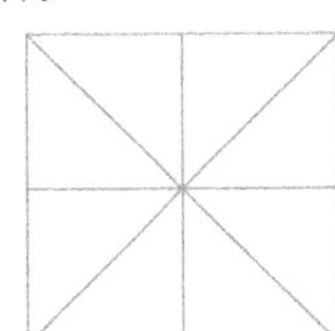

   (a) 10   (b) 8
   (c) 12   (d) 9

3. How many lines are there in the figure given below?

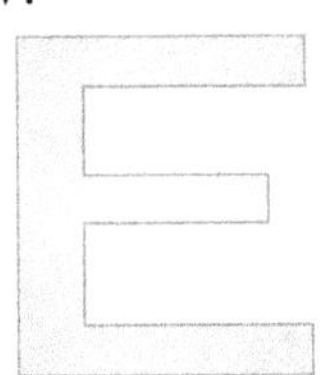

   (a) 10   (b) 12
   (c) 8   (d) 14

4. How many triangles are there in the given figure?

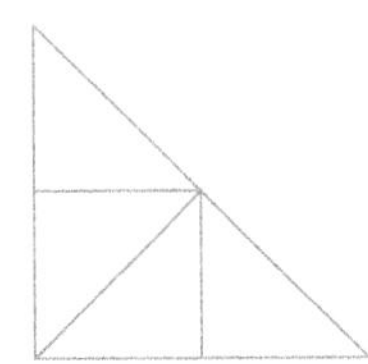

   (a) 10   (b) 8
   (c) 7   (d) 6

5. Count the number of triangles from the given complex figure.

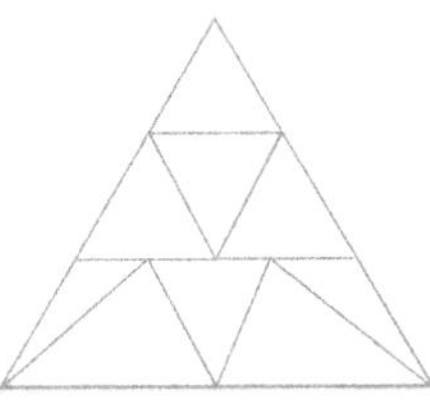

   (a) 11   (b) 10
   (c) 12   (d) 13

6. How many squares are there in the following figure?

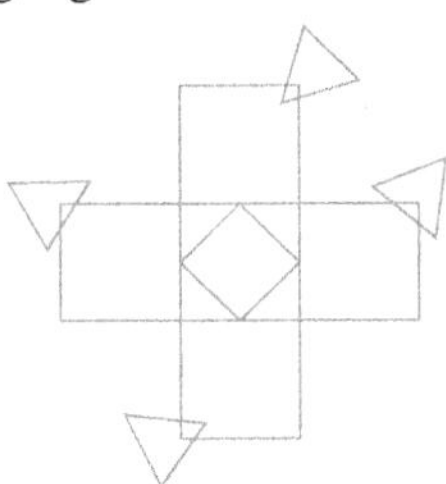

   (a) 5   (b) 8
   (c) 6   (d) 7

7. Count the number of squares in the given figure.

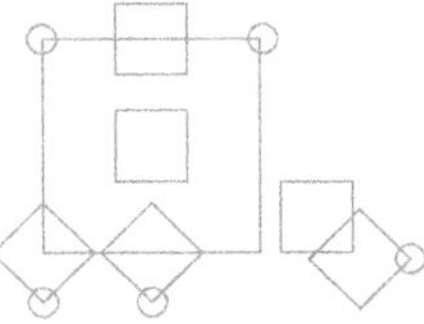

   (a) 9   (b) 6   (c) 7   (d) 8

8. How many squares are there in the given figure?

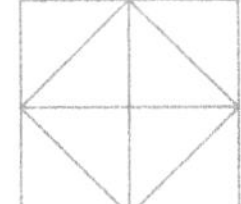

   (a) 6   (b) 8   (c) 5   (d) 4

9. How many circles are there in the given figure?

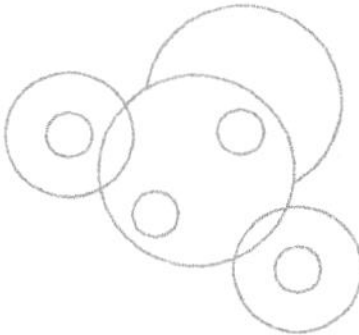

(a) 7   (b) 8   (c) 10   (d) 6

10. Find out the number of circles in the given figure.

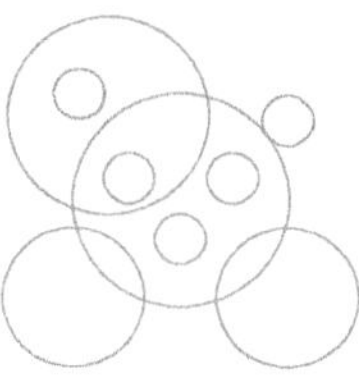

(a) 8   (b) 6   (c) 7   (d) 9

11. Count the number of circles in the given figure.

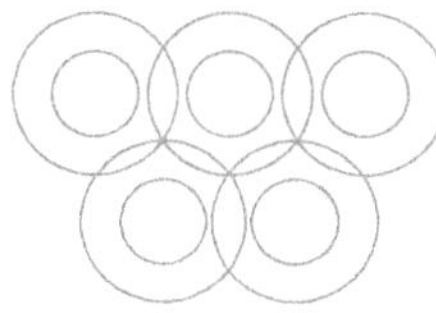

(a) 8   (b) 10   (c) 9   (d) 11

Directions (Q. Nos. 12 and 13) Answer the questions based on given figure.

12. How many different shapes are there in the figure?
(a) 2   (b) 5
(c) 3   (d) 4

13. How many circles are there in the figure?
(a) 10   (b) 9
(c) 8   (d) 7

14. Count the number of squares in the following figure.

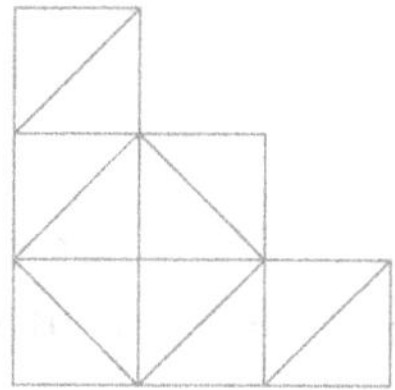

(a) 11   (b) 6
(c) 9   (d) 8

15. How many circles present in the given figures.

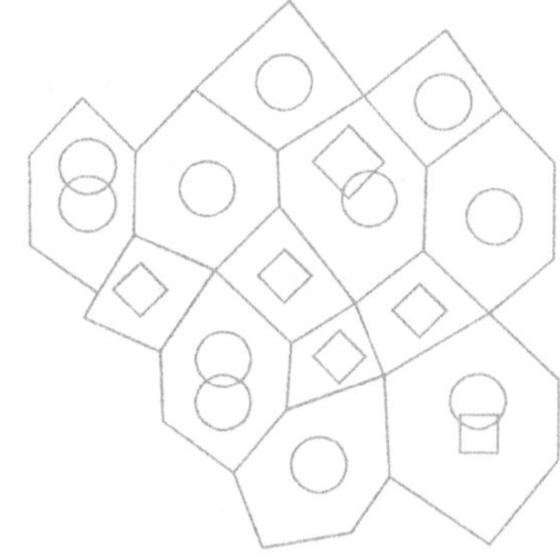

(a) 8   (b) 9
(c) 11   (d) 12

Chapter

09

Mirror Images

Mirror image is the image of a thing/person that appears when a mirror is placed vertically left or vertically right to in mirror images, the right part appears to be left and the left part appears to be right.

Mirror Images of Capital letters

Letters	A	B	C	D	E	F	G	H	I	J	K	L	M	N	O	P	Q	R	S	T	U	V	W	X	Y	Z
Mirror images	A	ᗺ	Ɔ	ᗡ	Ǝ	ꟻ	Ә	H	I	Ⴑ	ꓘ	⅃	M	И	O	ꟼ	Ϙ	Я	Ƨ	T	U	V	W	X	Y	ᘔ

Mirror Images of Numbers

Numbers	1	2	3	4	5	6	7	8	9
Mirror images	I	Ƨ	Ɛ	ᔨ	ꙅ	∂	ᒣ	8	ɘ

EXAMPLE 1 How the cartoon (X) will look when it is seen in the mirror?

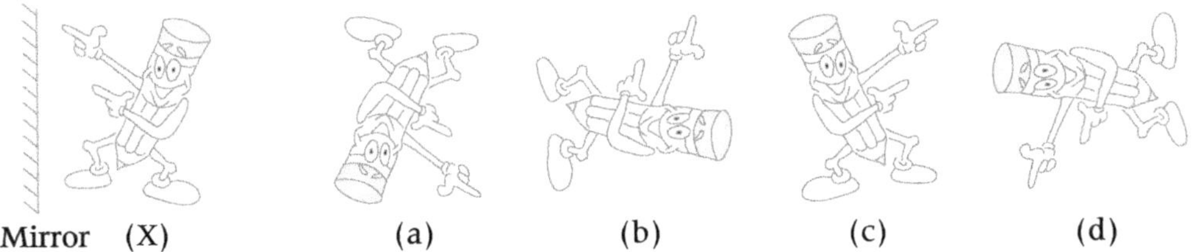

Mirror (X) (a) (b) (c) (d)

Sol. *(c)* As the mirror is placed on the left side of the cartoon. So, its left hand will appear as right hand and right hand will appear as its left hand as shown in the figure below

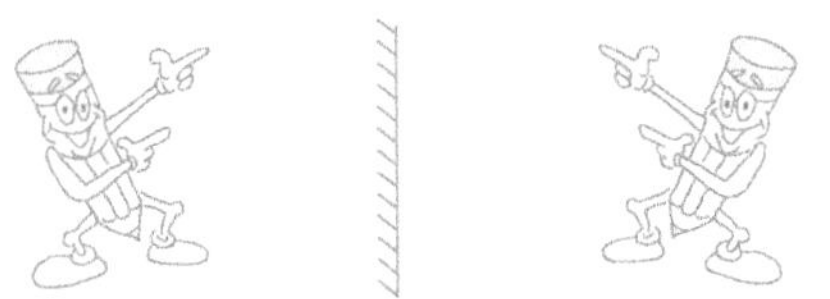

Mirror image Mirror Original image

Hence, option (c) is correct.

EXAMPLE 2   Find from the given alternatives the mirror image of the following figure (X), when the mirror is placed on the right side.

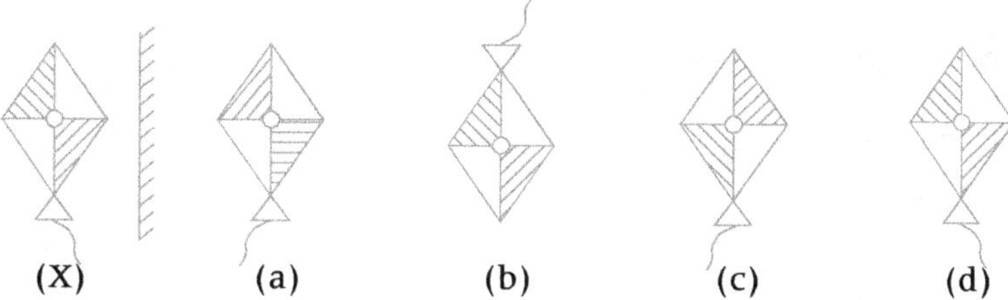

    (X)   (a)   (b)   (c)   (d)

Sol. *(c)* The mirror image of the kite will appear as shown in adjacent figure.

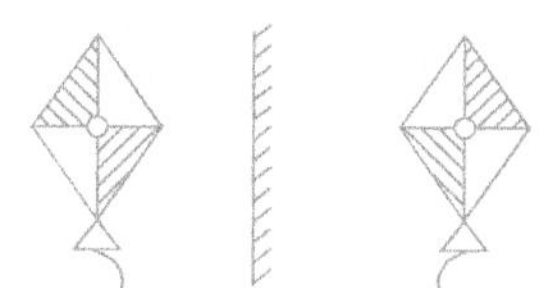

Original image   Mirror   Mirror image

Hence, option (c) is correct.

EXAMPLE 3   A child writes his name on a piece of paper and stands besides the mirror. How the letters of his name will appear in the mirror?

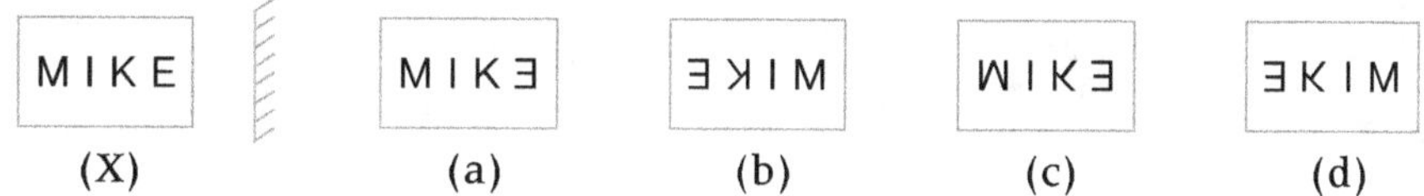

    (X)   (a)   (b)   (c)   (d)

Sol. *(b)* The name of child will appear as shown below

Original image   Mirror   Mirror image

Hence, option (b) is correct.

EXAMPLE 4   On an envelope ,the city code was written. How it will appear in the mirror, if it is kept on the left side of the mirror?

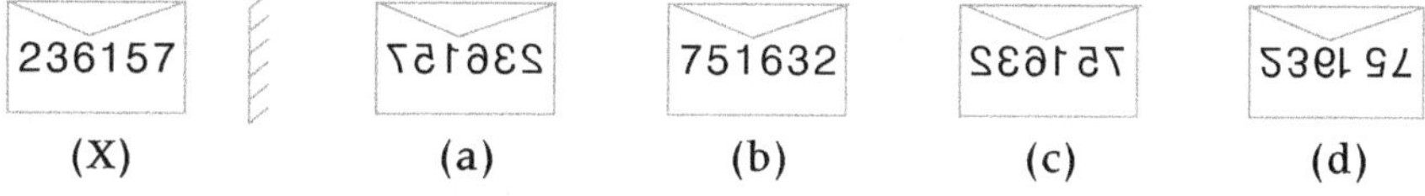

    (X)   (a)   (b)   (c)   (d)

Sol. *(a)* The number on the envelope will appear as shown below

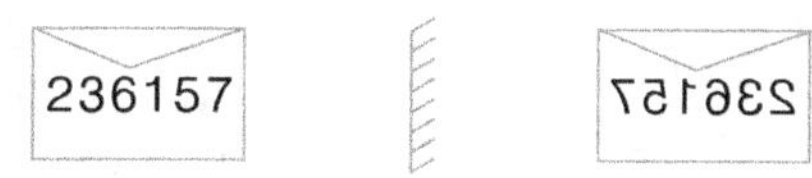

Original image   Mirror   Mirror image

Hence, option (a) is correct.

⏰ Let's Practice

1. Find the mirror image of the hockey stick and ball when the hockey stick and ball are kept on the right side of the mirror.

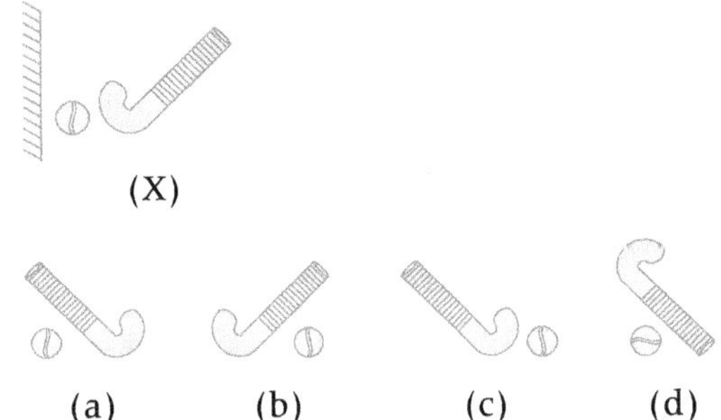

(X)

(a)   (b)   (c)   (d)

2. Micky Mouse cartoon was being telecasted on the television. A child was observing the Micky in the mirror. How micky will appear in the mirror?

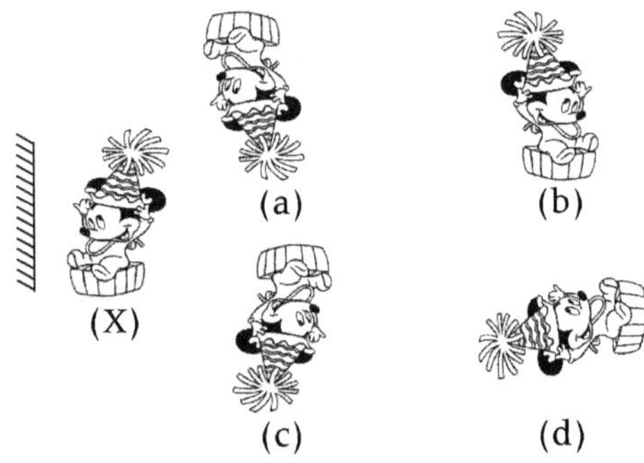

(X)   (a)   (b)   (c)   (d)

3. Find the mirror image of the figure (X) when the mirror is placed on the right side of the figure.

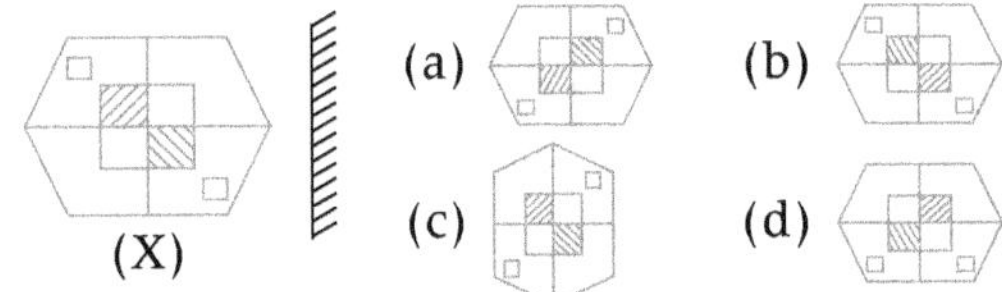

(X)   (a)   (b)   (c)   (d)

4. What will be the mirror image of the wall clock when the mirror is on the right side?

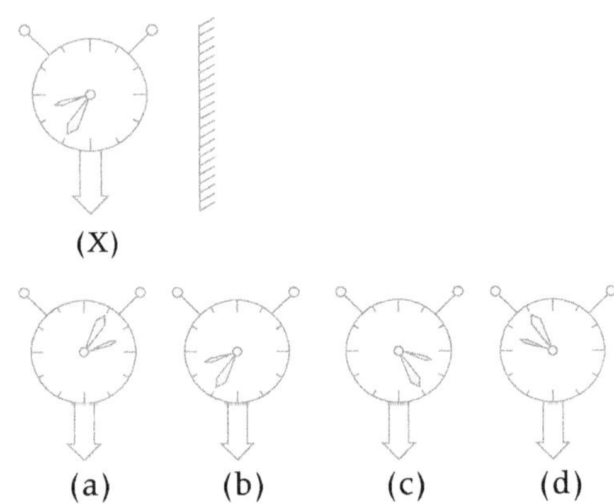

(X)

(a)   (b)   (c)   (d)

5. How will the arrows pointing to certain directions on the road will appear in the right mirror of the car?

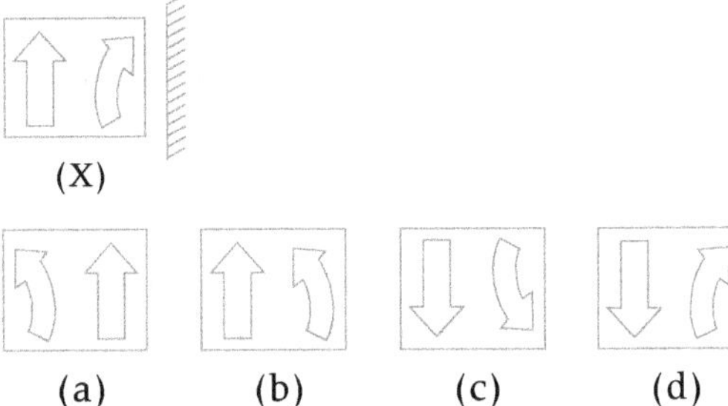

(X)

(a)   (b)   (c)   (d)

6. How the sponge bob will appear in the mirror, if the mirror is on the right side?

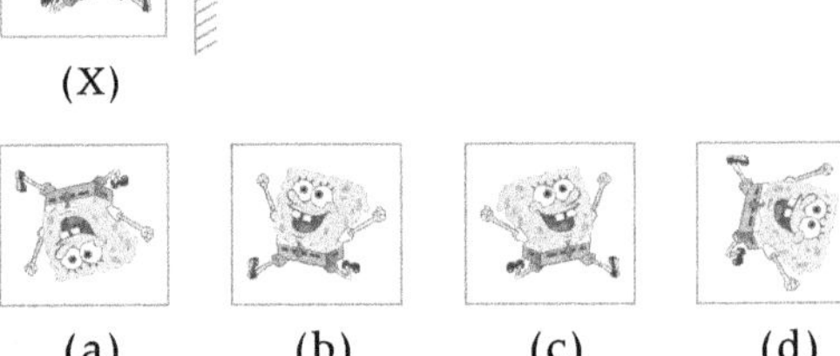

(X)

(a)   (b)   (c)   (d)

7. In a class, a picture was hanging on the right side of the wall. How will the picture appear in the mirror, if the mirror is placed on the left side of it?

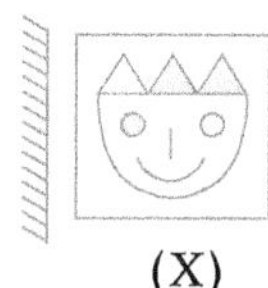
(X)

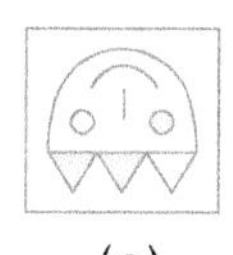   
(a)   (b)   (c)   (d)

8. A child draws the Donald Duck's picture on the drawing sheet and its mirror image. Which one from amongst the following will be the mirror image of the Donald Duck?

(X)

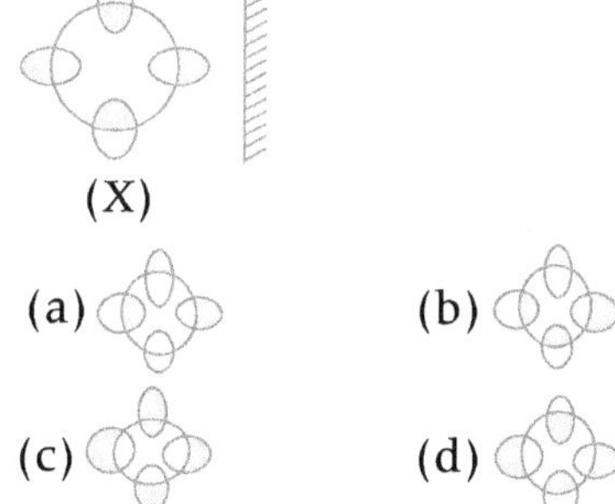
(a)   (b)   (c)   (d)

9. Find the mirror image of the following picture.

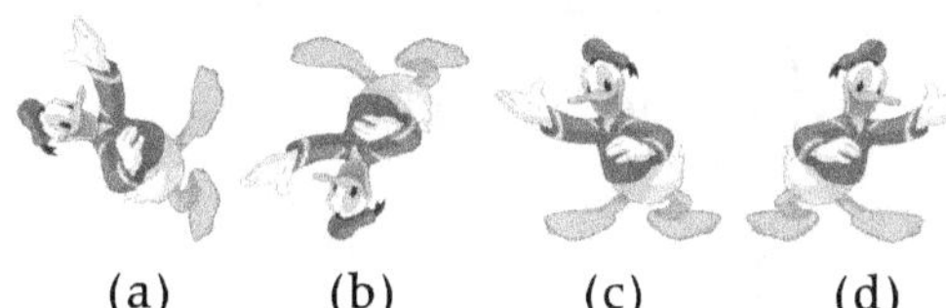
(X)   (a)   (b)   (c)   (d)

10. Find the mirror image of given figure (X).

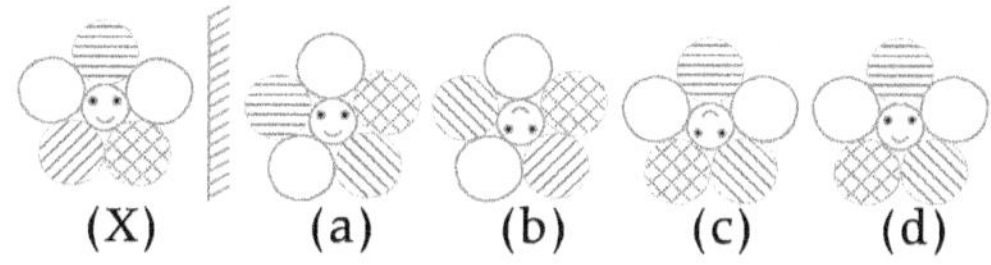
(X)

(a)   (b)

(c)   (d)

11. Find the mirror image of given figure (X).

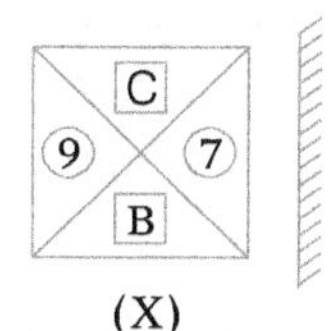
(X)

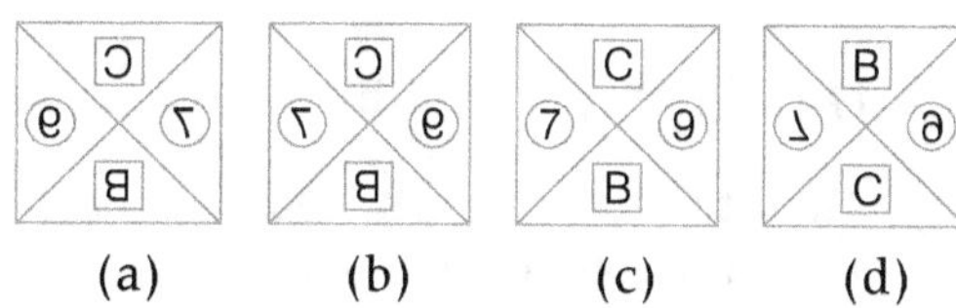
(a)   (b)   (c)   (d)

12. Find the mirror image of given figure (X).

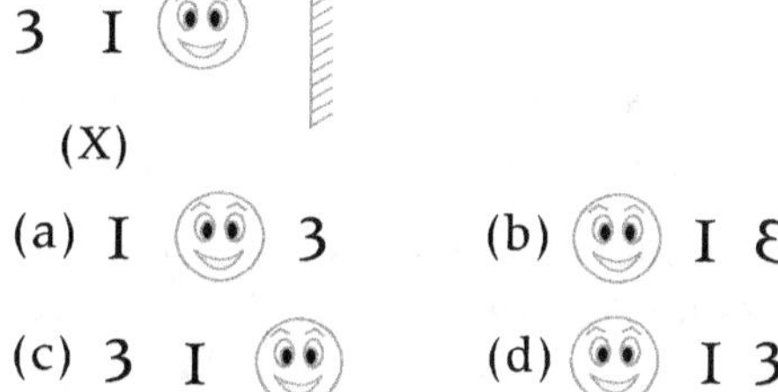
(X)

(a)   (b)

(c)   (d)

13. Find the mirror image of given figure (X).

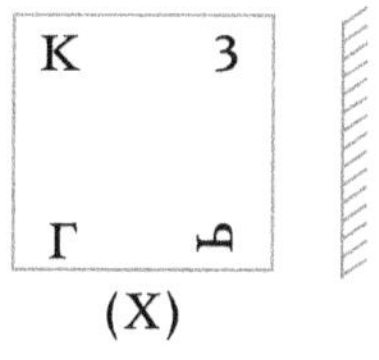
(X)

(a)   (b)

(c)   (d)

14. Find the mirror image of given word.

Q U I C K

(a) K Ɔ I U Ọ   (b) ꓘ Ɔ I U Ọ

(c) Ọ U I Ɔ K   (d) I C K U Ọ

15. A child writes the word 'SHARE' on a paper and stands besides the mirror. How the word will appear in the mirror, when the child is standing on the left side?

SHARE	ƎЯAHƧ	ƎЯAHƧ	ƎЯAHS	EЯAHƧ
(X)	(a)	(b)	(c)	(d)

16. How the letters of the word given will appear in the mirror, when the mirror is on the left side?

D A V I D

(X)

(a) D A V I ᗡ   (b) D I V A D

(c) D ∀ ∧ I D   (d) ᗡ I V A ᗡ

17. A number '614932' is written on the wall. How will it appear in the mirror, if the mirror is on the right side?

6 1 4 9 3 2

(X)

(a) 2 3 9 4 1 6   (b) 6 1 4 9 3 2

(c) 2 3 9 4 1 6   (d) 2 3 9 4 1 6

18. What will be the number seen in the mirror of the car?

7 5 2 9 8

(X)

(a) 7 5 2 9 8   (b) 8 9 2 5 7

(c) 8 9 2 5 7   (d) 8 6 2 5 7

19. Which of the following options shows the correct mirror image of the given combination?

← Q E 1 5 3 →

(X)

(a) → Ò E I 2 3 →   (b) ← Ɛ ƨ I Ǝ Ọ →

(c) ← Ɛ ƨ I Ǝ Ọ →   (d) → Q E I ƨ 3 ←

20. What will be the mirror image of clock time 4:40?

(a) 6:20   (b) 7:20

(c) 8:20   (d) 7:00

Chapter 10

Inserting the Missing Character

Inserting the missing character means filling up the empty space in the given shape using number/letter following some rules.

To understand it in a better way, let us consider the following example

EXAMPLE 1 A child while playing observes the following numbers and find one number missing. What will be the missing number?

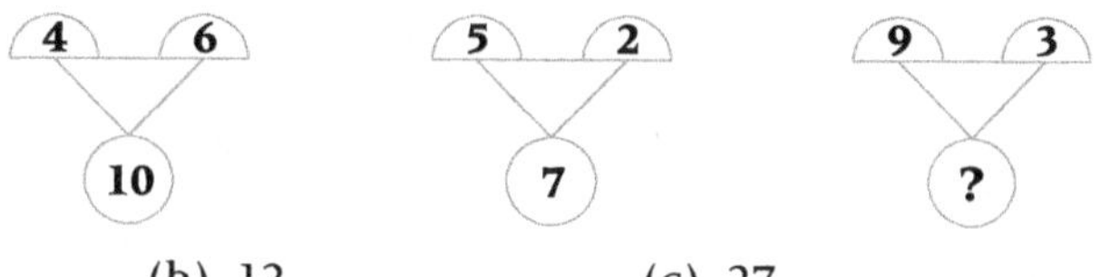

  (a) 10   (b) 12   (c) 27   (d) 16

Sol. *(b)* Number written in the circle is the sum of the numbers written in the semi-circles.

  As, $4 + 6 = 10$ and $5 + 2 = 7$ Similarly, $9 + 3 = \boxed{12}$

  Hence, option (b) is correct.

EXAMPLE 2 Liza drew some patterns and wrote some numbers in it. Find the missing number in the pattern.

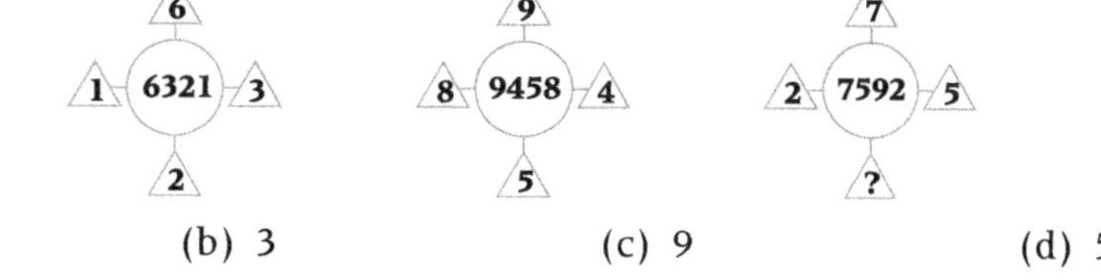

  (a) 6   (b) 3   (c) 9   (d) 5

Sol. *(c)* Same numbers appear in the circle and in the triangle.

  So, the missing number is 9. Hence, option (c) is correct.

EXAMPLE 3 On a circular sheet of paper, some numbers are written following a certain pattern. Find the missing number.

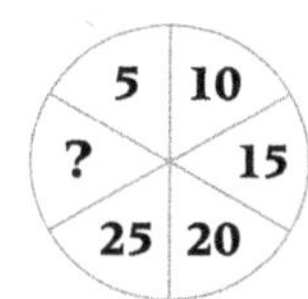

  (a) 40   (b) 23   (c) 35   (d) 30

Sol. *(d)* Starting from 5, 5 is added in each number to get the next number.

As, $5 + 5 = 10, 10 + 5 = 15, 15 + 5 = 20, 20 + 5 = 25$. So, $25 + 5 = \boxed{30}$

Hence, option (d) is correct.

EXAMPLE 4 Find the number which will come in place of question mark (?).

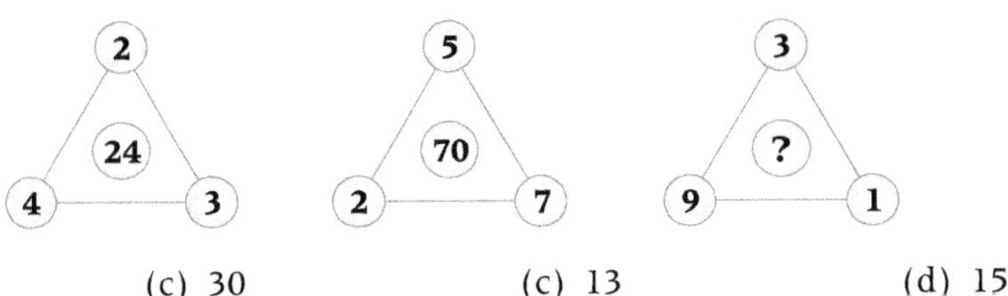

(a) 27   (c) 30   (c) 13   (d) 15

Sol. *(a)* The pattern is as follows:

As, $2 \times 4 \times 3 = 24$ and $5 \times 2 \times 7 = 70$ Similarly, $3 \times 9 \times 1 = \boxed{27}$

Hence, option (a) is correct.

EXAMPLE 5 Find the missing letter written on the sheet of paper.

P	D	G
Q	E	?
R	F	I

(a) H   (b) J   (c) K   (d) R

Sol. *(a)* In each column, consecutive letters are given. So, in the last column 'H' will be the missing letter.

Hence, option (a) is correct.

EXAMPLE 6 Certain blocks were arranged having a number and a letter on them. Find the missing number and letter.

	A1	
D4	E5	B2
	?	

(a) G7   (b) C3   (c) C6   (d) H8

Sol. *(b)* Each block consists of letter and its corresponding positional value in English alphabetical series.

As, $1 \to$ A (in English alphabet), $2 \to$ B, $\boxed{3} \to \boxed{\text{C}}$, $4 \to$ D and $5 \to$ E

So, the missing number and letter will be C3.

Hence, option (b) is correct.

Let's Practice

1. Which number from the given alternatives will replace the question mark (?) ?

8	18	26
7	9	16
11	7	?

(a) 19   (b) 17
(c) 20   (d) 18

2. The footballs consist of numbers based on some pattern. After observing the pattern, find the number which will replace the question mark (?).

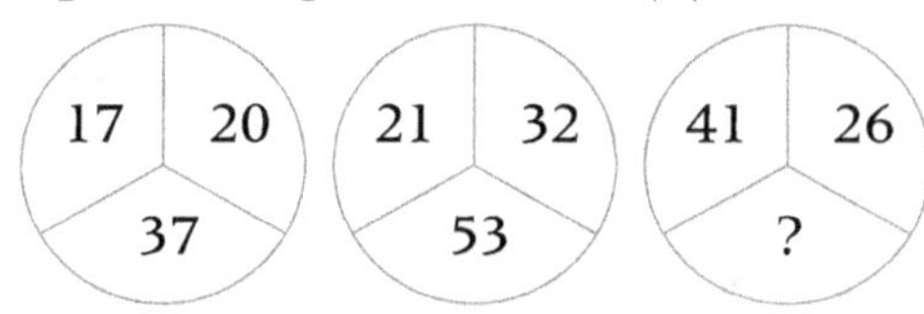

(a) 70   (b) 56
(c) 67   (d) 50

3. The given figures consist of numbers. Find the missing number.

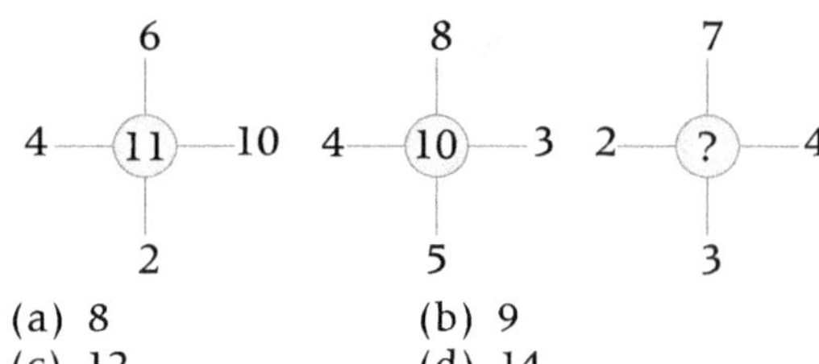

(a) 8   (b) 9
(c) 12   (d) 14

4. A child has three triangle shaped toys on which numbers are written and number on one toy is missing. Find that missing number.

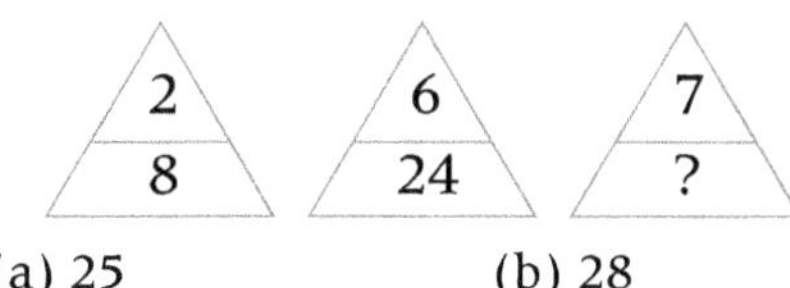

(a) 25   (b) 28
(c) 21   (d) 35

5. The given figures consist of numbers following a certain pattern. On the basis of the same pattern, find the missing number.

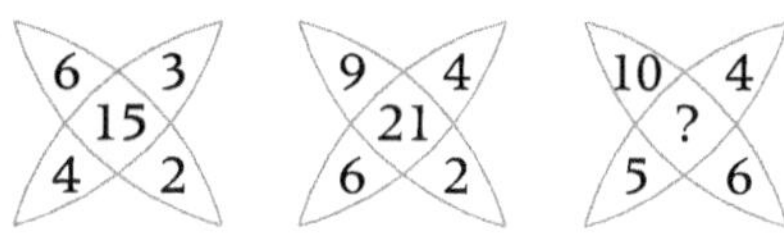

(a) 25   (b) 35
(c) 39   (d) 45

6. Find the number which will replace the question mark (?).

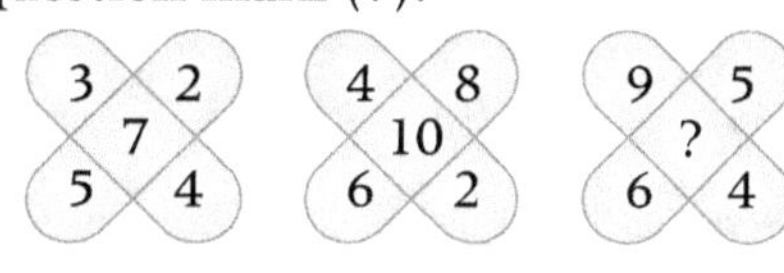

(a) 12   (b) 10
(c) 12   (d) 11

7. Felix has drawn a certain pattern in which numbers are written. Find the missing number.

2		3		5		2		1		6
	24				?				108	
4		1		3		4		2		9

(a) 154   (b) 132
(c) 160   (d) 120

8. The figures consist of three circles and numbers are written in it following some rule. Find the missing number following the same rule which others are following.

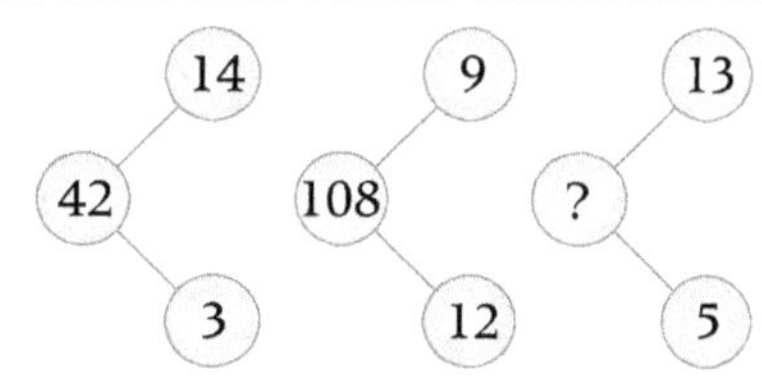

(a) 81   (b) 65
(c) 78   (d) 90

9. Rahul has three chocolates in the form of star. The price of each chocolate following a certain pattern. On the basis of the same pattern. Find the price of the third chocolate?

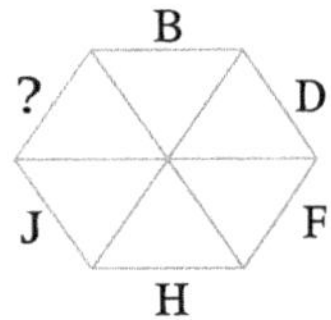

(a) ₹ 8

(b) ₹ 10

(c) ₹ 12

(d) ₹ 20

10. Find the missing letter in the given figure.

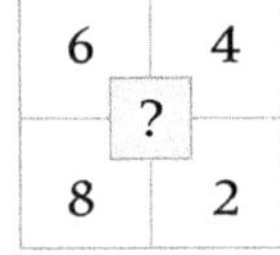

(a) M   (b) K

(c) L   (d) P

11. The table given below consists of letters. Which letter will replace the question mark (?)?

A	B	C
C	D	E
F	?	H

(a) E   (b) I

(c) G   (d) J

12. Suhani has drawn a certain pattern in which alphabets are written. Find the missing alphabet?

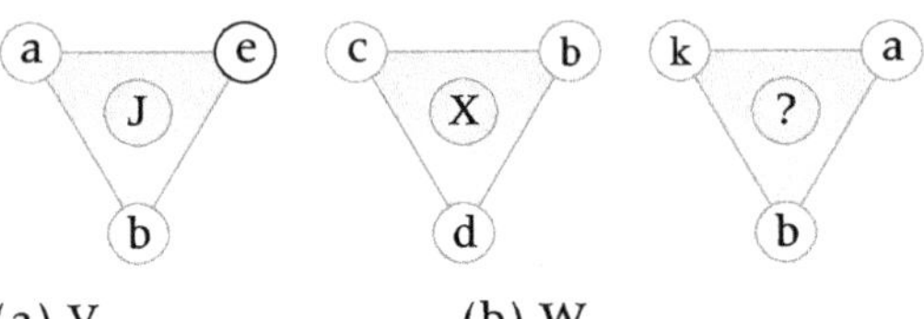

(a) V   (b) W

(c) U   (d) T

13. The given below kite shape structures consist of numbers and letters. Find the missing number in it.

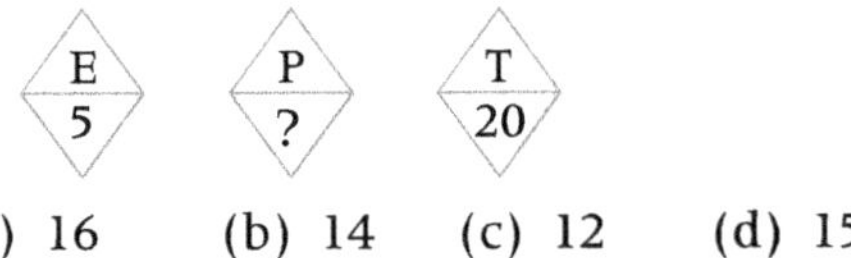

(a) 16   (b) 14   (c) 12   (d) 15

14. The given figures consist of numbers and letters. Find the missing letter in it.

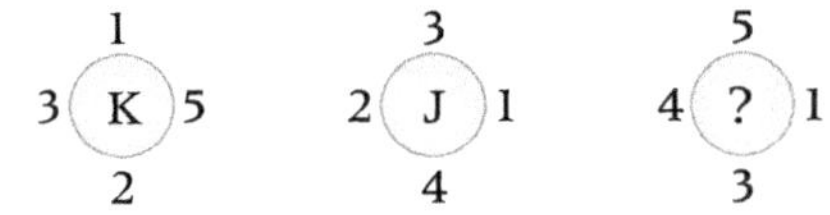

(a) N   (b) M

(c) O   (d) L

15. Find the missing character which replace the question mark(?).

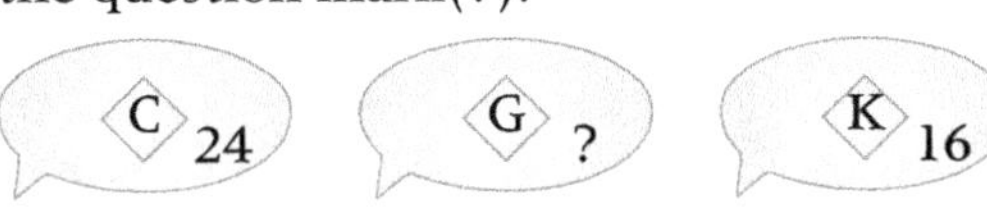

(a) 20   (b) 21

(c) 19   (d) 7

Position and Comparison Test

Ranking means determining the position of a person/object in a row/queue.

Let us consider the following example to understand how we find out the rank of a person in a row.

EXAMPLE 1 In a group photograph, five friends were standing as shown in the picture given below. What is Harry's rank from the left end?

    (a) 2nd   (b) 3rd   (c) 4th   (d) 5th

Sol. *(b)* As we observe the above picture, Harry's rank is 3rd from the left end of the row, when we count his position taking our left side.
Hence, option (b) is correct.

In 'ranking test', following types of questions are generally asked

EXAMPLE 2 Some men were standing in a line waiting for the Railway ticket window to open. There are 4 people ahead of Jonas and 3 people behind him. What was Jonas's rank from the start.

    (a) 3rd   (b) 6th   (c) 4th   (d) 5th

Sol. *(d)* Jonas's rank from the ticket window is 5th as we count from the starting.
Hence, option (d) is correct.

EXAMPLE 3 In a building of 15 floors. Mr. Paul lives on 6th floor from the bottom. Find on which floor he lives from the top?

 (a) 10th   (b) 12th   (c) 9th   (d) 8th

Sol. (a) The floor on which Mr. Paul lives can be shown as follows:

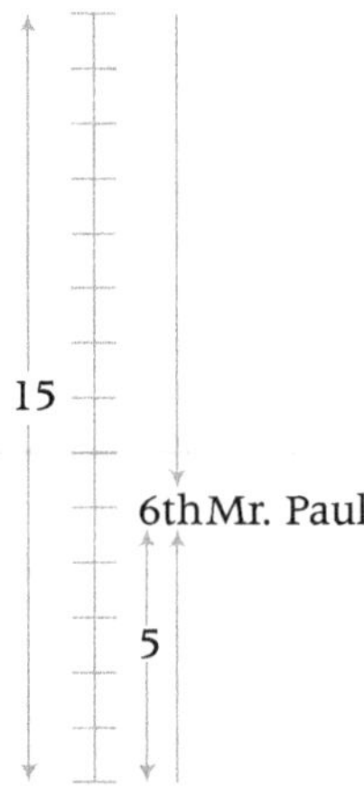

When we count it from the top to bottom, Mr. Paul lives on 10th floor from the top.
Hence, option (a) is correct.

EXAMPLE 4 In a row of girls, Nina is ranked 15th from the left end and 20th from the right end. How many girls are there in the row?

 (a) 35   (b) 34   (c) 30   (d) 20

Sol. (b) In a row, the girls can be arranged as follows

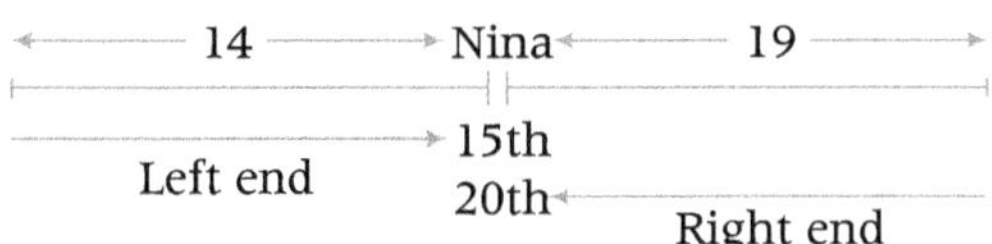

There are 14 girls before Nina and 19 girls after Nina and one Nina herself.
So, total number of girls in the row = 14 + 19 + 1 = 34.
Hence option (b) is correct.

EXAMPLE 5 Priti scored more than Rahul, Rahul scored more than Yamuna and Manju scored more than Priti, who scored the lowest?

 (a) Priti   (b) Yamuna   (c) Rahul   (d) Manju

Sol. (b) According to the question,

$$\text{Priti} > \text{Rahul}$$
$$\text{Rahul} > \text{Yamuna}$$
$$\text{Manju} > \text{Priti}$$

(here we used symbol ($>$) for more than) or we can arranged as,

$$\text{Manju} > \text{Priti} > \text{Rahul} > \boxed{\text{Yamuna}}$$

So, it is clear from the above arrangement, Yamuna scored lowest among them.
Hence, option (b) is correct.

⏰ Let's Practice

1. Five stars of different colours were hanging in a string. Which colour star will be 4th from the bottom in the string?

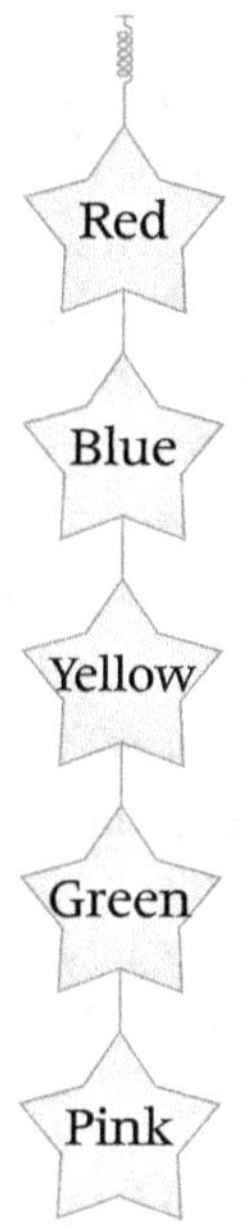

  (a) Red   (b) Yellow
  (c) Blue   (d) Green

Directions (Q. Nos. 2 and 3) Answer the questions based on the given information.

Eight friends went to the zoo. While entering the zoo, they were in a queue as shown below.

2. How many friends will be behind Leon, if 3 more friends join them?
  (a) 3   (b) 5
  (c) 4   (d) 6

3. If Hans and Laura interchange their positions. How many friends are there between Laura and Tim?
  (a) 2   (b) 3
  (c) 5   (d) 4

4. Ricky and Sharne are standing in a line waiting for the train. When the train arrives, Ricky will be the 3rd to get in and Sharne will be 7th. How many persons are standing between Ricky and Sharne?
  (a) 2   (b) 3
  (c) 5   (d) 2

5. In a row of students, Leah is 13th from left end and George is 10th from right end. If 35 students are there in a row, then how many students are there between Leah and George?
  (a) 10   (b) 9
  (c) 8   (d) 12

6. 9 girls took part in a fashion show. They are standing in the queue as shown below. If Pixie is 4th from the left end. What will be her position from the right end?

  (a) 5th   (b) 7th
  (c) 6th   (d) 8th

44

7. In a cricket stadium, Neo was sitting on 8th stair from the top. If there are 30 stairs, then on which stair Neo was sitting from the bottom?
   (a) 22nd (b) 20th (c) 23rd (d) 25th

8. In a train, Mitul was sitting in 8th coach from the right while travelling to Kerala. If there are 20 coaches in all, then what will be the position of the coach from the left in which Mitul is sitting?
   (a) 13th (b) 15th (c) 14th (d) 12th

9. Some boys are standing in a line. Bryan is 13th from one end and 16th from the other. How many boys are standing in the line?
   (a) 28 (b) 29 (c) 25 (d) 30

10. Some chairs of different colours are arranged in a queue. Red colour chair is 10th from the left end and 16th from the right end. How many chairs are there in the queue?
    (a) 25   (b) 26
    (c) 28   (d) 30

11. If Liza is 4th from left end and Nio is 6th from right end and 3 girls are between them, then number of girls in the row is
    (a) 13   (b) 15
    (c) 16   (d) 12

12. Sheena is taller than Nami and shorter than Lim only. Nami is not the shortest. Lim is taller than Kian. Who is the shortest?
    (a) Kian   (b) Nami
    (c) Sheena   (d) Lim

13. Priyanshi is taller than Ashok and Ashok is taller than Jitu. Motu is the tallest. Find out who is the shortest.
    (a) Jitu
    (b) Motu
    (c) Priyanshi
    (d) Ashok

14. I. Yami, Gautam, Avani, Lovely take a series of test.
    II. No two students get similar marks.
    III. Yami always score more than lovely.
    IV. Avani score more than Yami.
    V. Gautam score less than Lovely.
    Find out who scored highest.
    (a) Yami   (b) Gautam
    (c) Lovely   (d) Avani

15. There is a ice-cream parlour. The ice-cream seller told that Vanilla ice-cream is bigger than the Coconut ice-cream. Chocolate ice-cream is bigger than the Vanilla ice-cream but smaller than Mango ice-cream. Which of the following is the correct order of ice-cream from the biggest to the smallest?

Chocolate Mango   Vanilla   Coconut
ice-cream ice-cream ice-cream ice-cream

(a) Vanilla, Coconut, Chocolate, Mango
(b) Mango, Chocolate, Coconu, Vanilla
(c) Mango, Vanilla, Chocolate, Coconut
(d) Mango, Chocolate, Vanilla, Coconut

Chapter 12

Find Direction

The four directions we usually know are East, West, North and South and they are called main directions.

The main directions can be shown with the help of the diagram below.

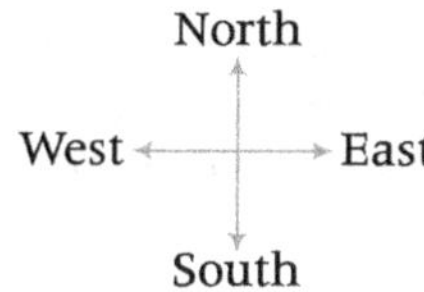

Now, we will discuss the four sub-directions.

Sub-directions are the directions between two consecutive main directions, i.e. North-East, South-East, South-West and North-West.

The four sub-directions can be shown as

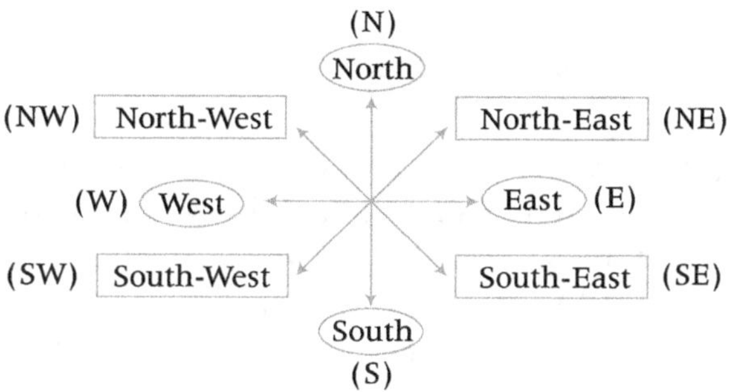

EXAMPLE 1   A teacher standing in the class faces the West direction towards the students sitting in the class and scold them to look towards the board pointing her hands. In which direction, the teacher's hands are pointing?

(a) East   (b) West   (c) North   (d) South

Sol. *(a)* From the above picture, we get that the board is in East direction and the teacher's hands are pointing also in East direction.
Hence, option (a) is correct.

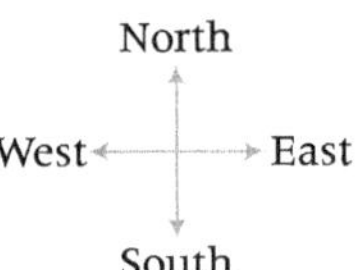

EXAMPLE 2 Liza walks towards East, after travelling some distance she takes a left turn and again after travelling some distance she turns to left. In which direction she is facing now?

(a) North   (b) East   (c) West   (d) South

Sol. *(c)* Liza's movements are as follow :

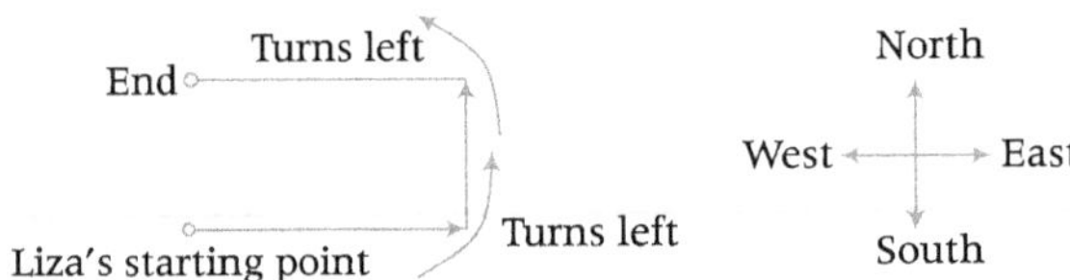

When we compare the above drawn direction diagram with the standard direction diagram, we observe that, Liza is facing in West direction.

Hence, option (c) is correct.

EXAMPLE 3 City D is to the West of city M. City R is to the South of city D. If city K is to the East of city R, then in which direction is city K located in respect of city D?

(a) North   (b) East   (c) North-East   (d) South-East

Sol. *(d)* According to the question, the direction diagram is as follows

So, city K is located in the South-East direction.
Hence, option (d) is correct.

EXAMPLE 4 A man starts from his house and walked straight for 10m towards North and turned left and walked 25m. He then turned right and walked 5m and again turned right and walked 25m. How far is he from his original position?

(a) 5m   (b) 10m   (c) 15m   (d) 25m

Sol. *(c)* According to the question, the diagram will be as follows

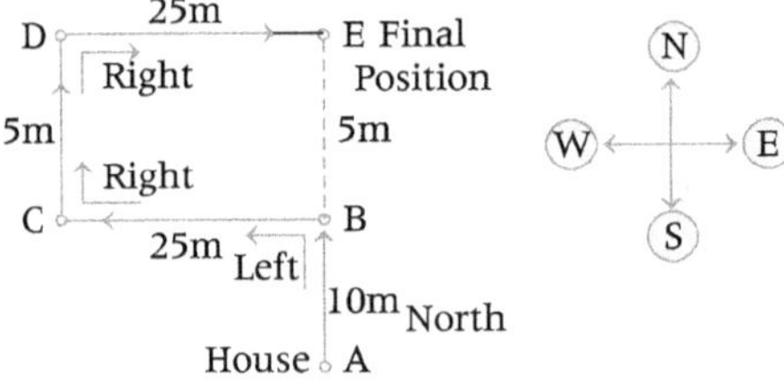

From his original position $(AE) = AB + BE$

$$AB = 10m \Rightarrow BE = ?$$

$$CD = BE = 5m \Rightarrow AE = AB + BE = 10 + 5 = 15m$$

Hence, option (c) is correct.

⏰ Let's Practice

1. While facing in South direction, Marry's right hand is in West direction, her left hand is in East direction, then her back will be in which direction?

  (a) South   (b) East
  (c) West   (d) North

2. The time in clock is 12 : 15 as shown in the clock below. In which direction, is the minute hand face?

  (a) East   (b) West   (c) North (d) South

3. Martin faces towards South while standing on the road as he has been lost in the market and don't know in which direction to go to reach his house. His house is to his right hand. In which direction, his house is from his present position?

  (a) West   (b) North-East
  (c) North   (d) East

4. There are four roads. I have come from South and want to go to city B. The road to the right goes to city D and road to the left goes to city B while straight road goes to city M. In which direction, is the city B?

  (a) North (b) East   (c) West (d) South

5. Pranvi is facing the city mall. She makes a $\frac{3}{4}$ turn to the right. Where will she be facing now?

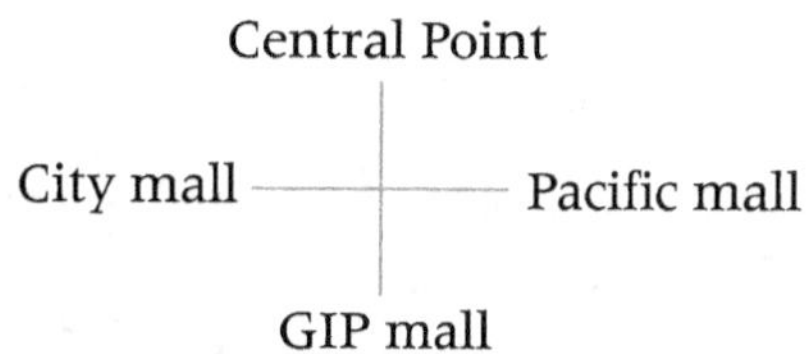

  (a) Central point
  (b) Pacific mall
  (c) City mall
  (d) GIP mall

6. In a park, there are eight trees which are as shown below

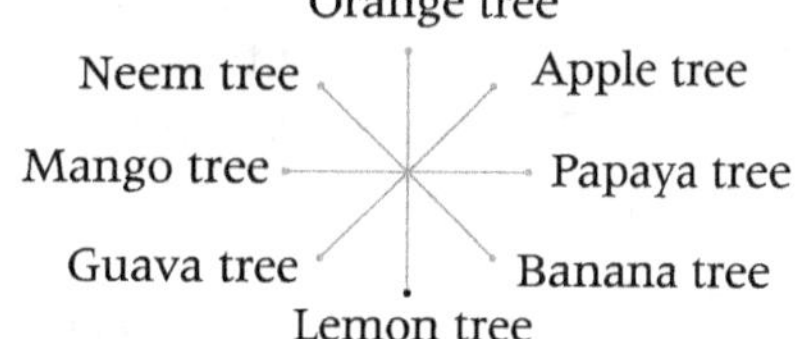

Lemon tree is in which direction from the orange tree?

  (a) East   (b) West
  (c) North   (d) South

7. Paul was standing on the road heading towards East. The arrows on the pole depict two directions as shown in the picture below. Paul wants to go to cafe. Now, in which direction he must go to reach cafe?

  (a) West   (b) North (c) East (d) South

8. Mall is towards the North of Library. Temple is towards the West of Mall. Railway Station is towards the South of Temple. In which direction, Railway Station is from the Library?
   (a) North
   (b) East
   (c) West
   (d) South

9. If Harry's house is located to the South of Karl's house and George's house is to the East of Karl's house. In which direction, Harry's house is situated with respect to George's house?
   (a) North-East   (b) South-West
   (c) North-West   (d) South-East

10. Sophie's house is in East direction from her school. In the morning before going to school she first goes to church, then to school. Church is in South direction from her house. In which direction, the church is from the school?

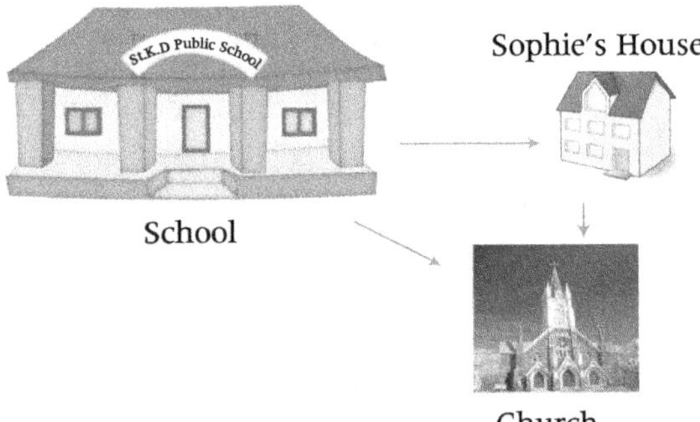

   (a) South
   (b) West
   (c) North-West
   (d) South-East

11. Shivam is going to science exhibition with his mother. He is facing towards. Snow fluff and then turns 1/7 anti-clockwise then what will he be facing?

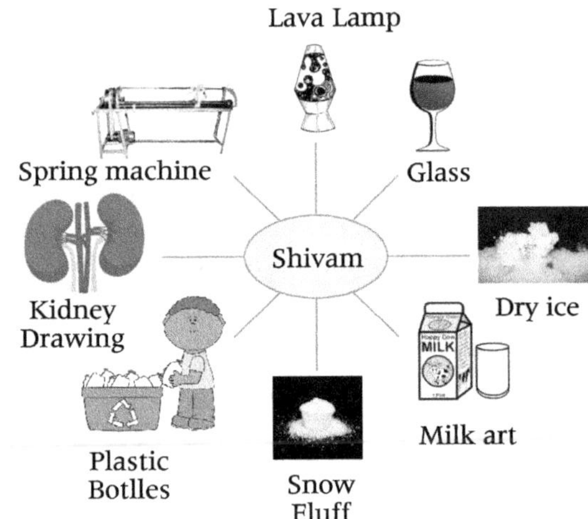

   (a) Plastic bottles   (b) Kidney drawing
   (c) Dry Ice   (d) Milk art

12. A cardboard has 16 square blocks. Some points are marked on it. Which point is in the North-West direction of point A?

D	E	F	
	A		
			M
N	O		

   (a) D   (b) N
   (c) F   (d) O

13. Harper wants to go to the M.K. theatre to watch the movie. He starts travelling towards North direction. After walking some distance he turns right, then turns left and again turns right and reaches M. K. theatre. In which direction, M. K. theatre is situated?
   (a) East   (b) West
   (c) North   (d) South

14. Lina comes out from her house and goes towards East direction, then turns left. She walks some distance and then turns towards her right. In which direction, is she facing now?
   (a) North   (b) East
   (c) West   (d) South

15. Joy is playing football in the playground. He faces in the East direction. From there, he turns left kicks the football straight towards North direction. Now, he goes near to the football, then turns right and kicks the football straight towards East direction. He again goes near to the football turns left and kicks the football straight. Now, in which direction Joy must go to kick the ball again?
    (a) South
    (b) North
    (c) East
    (d) West

16. Doraemon wants to meet his friend Nobita. So, he follows a particular path in South direction, then he turns towards left and travels for some distance. After that he turns right and moves certain distance. At last he turns left and travels again for some distance and meet Nobita. Find out which of the following shows the correct path travelled by Doraemon?

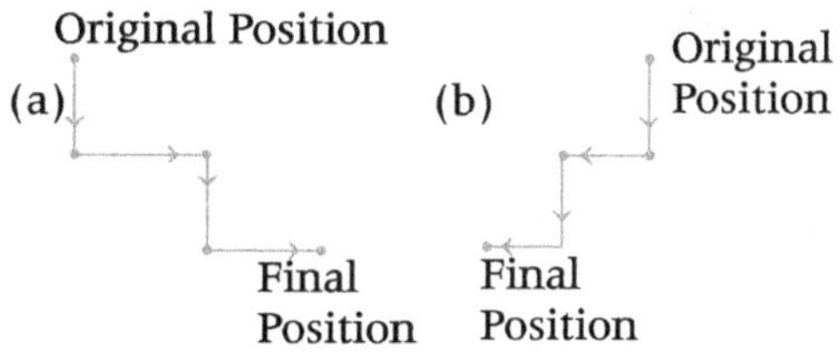

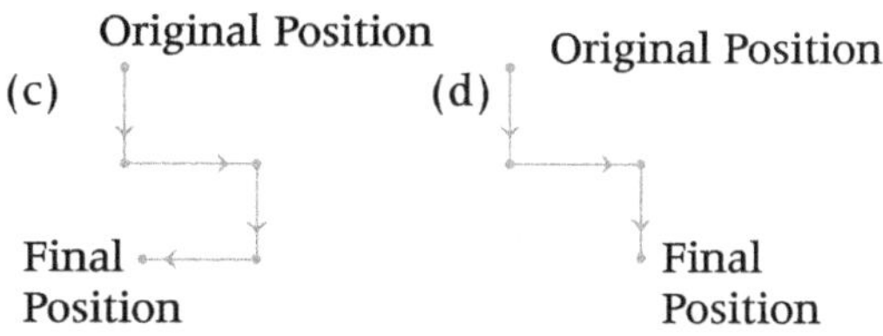

Directions (Q. Nos. 17 and 18) Use the diagram below to answer the following questions.

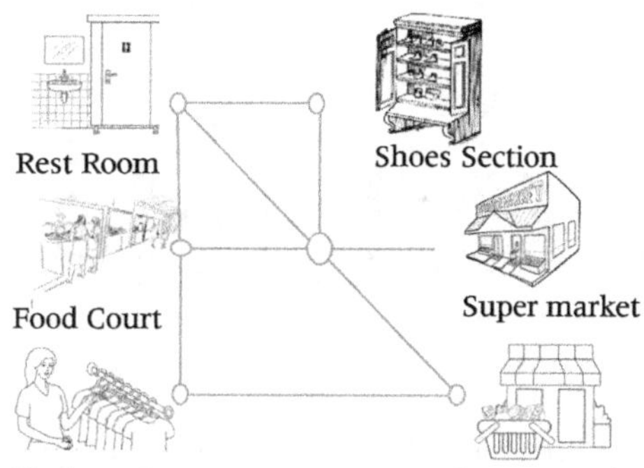

17. Cloth section is in .... of grocery section.
    (a) East   (b) West
    (c) North   (d) South

18. Restroom is in ...... of foodcourt section.
    (a) North   (b) South
    (c) North-East   (d) South-West

19. Mona walks 30 m in South. Then, she turns right and walks 20 m. Now, she turns right and walks 30 m. How far is she from her original position?
    (a) 15 m   (b) 30 m
    (c) 20 m   (d) 45 m

20. Observe the following diagram and answer the following question

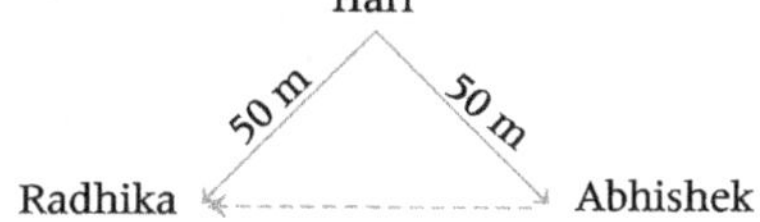

Radhika is 50 m South-West of Hari. Abhishek is 50 m South-East of Hari, then Radhika is in which direction of Abhishek?
    (a) North-West   (b) South-West
    (c) East   (d) West

Calendar Knowledge

A calendar is a systematic arrangement of day, week and month in a defined patterns. With the help of calendar we can easily recognise the required date, month or week of a particular day.

The Indian National calendar contains the following

1. Day and Date   2. Week   3. Month   4. Year

Day and Date

A day is the 7th part of a week. It has 24 hours. It is the smallest unit of a calendar.

While a date is a reference to a particular day.

Week

A week is the 52nd part of a year. It is a grouping of 7 days.

 (i) Sunday   (ii) Monday   (iii) Tuesday   (iv) Wednesday

(v) Thursday   (vi) Friday   (vii) Saturday

Month

Months	Day	Months	Day
January	31 days	July	31 days
February	28 days (Ordinary year) 29 days (Leap year)	August	31 days
		September	30 days
March	31 days	October	31 days
April	30 days	November	30 days
May	31 days	December	31 days
June	30 days		

A month is the 12th part of a year. It has 28/29/30/31 days.

Year

A year has 12 month, which we already describe in Month.

Year has 2 type

1. **Ordinary or Normal Year** An ordinary year which has 365 days. Such year are not divisible by 4.
   ex. 2001, 2002, 2019, etc.

2. **Leap Year** A leap year is a year which has 366 days. Such years are exactly divisible by 4.
   ex. 800, 1200, 1600, 2000 etc.
   Lets have a look on following examples :

Directions (Ex. Nos. 1-3) Read the calendar and answer the following questions.

January 2004

Sun	Mon	Tue	Wed	Thu	Fri	Sat
	1	2	3	4	5	6
7	8	9	10	11	12	13
14	15	16	17	18	19	20
21	22	23	24	25	26	27
28	29	30	31			

EXAMPLE 1 How many days are there in January?

(a) 30   (b) 31   (c) 29   (d) 28

Sol. *(b)* According to given calendar January 2004, there are 31 days. Hence, option (b) is correct.

EXAMPLE 2 What will be the day of 31st January 2004?

(a) Tuesday   (b) Thursday   (c) Wednesday   (d) Sunday

Sol. *(c)* According to given calendar January 2004 on 31st January is Wednesday.

Hence, option (c) is correct.

EXAMPLE 3 Which day is just before 26th January?

(a) Thursday   (b) Saturday   (c) Wednesday   (d) Sunday

Sol. *(a)* According to given calendar, day just before 26th January is Thursday. Hence option (a) is correct.

EXAMPLE 4 If yesterday was Tuesday, what day will be the next day from today?

(a) Wednesday   (b) Friday   (c) Saturday   (d) Thursday

Sol. *(d)*

Yesterday	Today	Tomorrow (Next day)
Tuesday	Wednesday	Thursday

Hence, option (d) is correct.

EXAMPLE 5 Rohan correctly remembers that Priya's birthday was after Monday but before Thursday, Vishnu correctly remembers that Priya's birthday was after Tuesday but before Saturday, on which day of the week does Priya's birthday definitely fall?

    (a) Friday   (b) Tuesday

    (c) Wednesday   (d) Saturday

Sol. *(c)* According to Rohan Priya's birthday fall = Tuesday or Wednesday

According to Vishnu Priya's birthday fall = Wednesday , Thursday, Friday.

So, Priya's birthday falls on Wednesday.

Hence, option (c) is correct.

EXAMPLE 6 Tanu's principal wants to meet Tanu's parents. Meeting schedule on 16th July. 2 July is Monday, on which day of the week is meeting schedule.

    (a) Monday   (b) Tuesday   (c) Wednesday   (d) Saturday

Sol. *(a)* July 2 is Monday.

$$2 + 7 = 9 \text{ th will be Monday.}$$
$$9 + 7 = 16 \text{ th will be Monday.}$$

Hence, option (a) is correct.

🕐 Let's Practice

1. The month with neither 31 nor 30 days is?
   (a) May   (b) July
   (c) January   (d) February

2. Mona wanted to travel around the world. She worked it out that the trip would take her 6 years. How many months would that be?
   (a) 60 months   (b) 72 months
   (c) 12 months   (d) 6 months

3. If yesterday was Thursday, what day will be the 4th day from today?
   (a) Sunday   (b) Tuesday
   (c) Saturday   (d) Monday

4. Varnika remember her mother's birthday falls after Tuesday but before Friday. Varun correctly remember that his mother's birthday was after Wednesday but before Sunday. On which day of the week does mother's birthday fall?
   (a) Thursday   (b) Monday
   (c) Tuesday   (d) Friday

5. Tom started some work on Sunday. He promised to Jerry that he will complete the whole work in 8 days. His work will complete on ………. .
   (a) Sunday   (b) Monday
   (c) Tuesday   (d) Wednesday

6. Krishna correctly remembers that date of his Fancy dress competition falls after 13th August and before 17th August. His friend correctly remembers that the date is an odd number. What will be the date of Ayaan's dance competition?
   (a) 14th August   (b) 16th August
   (c) 13th August   (d) 15th August

7. In a video game shop, a gift box is free when someone won continuously 3 chances of any game played by he/she. On which day player get a chance to win the gift box.

Days	Video game
Wed	Super Mario
Sun	Pokemon
Friday	The Legend of Zelda
Mon	Free gift box
Sat	Bike racing

(a) Ist day of week   (b) 2nd day of week
(c) 4th day of week   (d) 6th day of week

8. Dhyanchand Hockey competition was held for three days before 3rd Saturday of August 20XX. The date on which Dhyanchand Hockey Competition started was ………. .

			August 20XX			
Sun	Mon	Tue	Wed	Thu	Fri	Sat
	1	2	3	4	5	6
7	8	9	10	11	12	13
14	15	16	17	18	19	20
21	22	23	24	25	26	27
28	29	30	31			

(a) 19th August   (b) 15th August
(c) 17th August   (d) 20th August

Directions (Q.Nos. 9-11) Read the calendar and answer the following questions.

			January 2021			
Sun	Mon	Tue	Wed	Thu	Fri	Sat
					①	2
3	4	5	6	7	8	9
10	11	12	13	14	15	16
17	18	⑲	20	21	22	23
24	25	26	27	28	29	30
31						

19 → A.P.J Abdul Kalam's Birthday

9. Which day is falling after two days of A.P.J Abdul Kalam's birthday?
(a) Wednesday   (b) Thursday
(c) Sunday   (d) Friday

10. How many working days are there in this month?
(a) 28   (b) 29
(c) 26   (d) 30

11. How many Sunday are there in this month?
(a) 5   (b) 4   (c) 3   (d) 6

12. Charly's birthday falls just after 4th Thursday of October 20XX. The day on which Charly's celebrates his birthday is ________ ?

			October 20XX			
Sun	Mon	Tue	Wed	Thu	Fri	Sat
			1	2	3	4
5	6	7	8	9	10	11
12	13	14	15	16	17	18
19	20	21	22	23	24	25
26	27	28	29	30	31	

(a) 23rd October
(b) 30th October
(c) 24th October
(d) 31th October

13. Gauri went to the dancing classes in June 20XX. If each Sunday and odd Saturday are holidays, then, for How many days did he go to the dancing classes.

			June 20XX			
Sun	Mon	Tue	Wed	Thu	Fri	Sat
	1	2	3	4	5	6
7	8	9	10	11	12	13
14	15	16	17	18	19	20
21	22	23	24	25	26	27
28	29	30				

(a) 26   (b) 25   (c) 24   (d) 27

PRACTICE SET 

1. Identify the one that does not belong to the group.
   (a) Water   (b) Jelly   (c) Coffee   (d) Milk

2. The given letters form a series. Select that letter from the given alternative which will continue the given series.

   L N P R T ?

   (a) U   (b) V   (c) W   (d) Y

3. Find the letter which will end the first word and start the second word.

   SHAR?ARS

   (a) P   (b) Y   (c) B   (d) E

4. Rover stands 6th from the left end in a queue of 15 persons at the bus stop. What will be his position from the right end in the queue?
   (a) 8th   (b) 9th   (c) 10th   (d) 11th

5. Mixi observed a pattern on a sheet of paper from which, pattern at the corner was missing. Find that missing pattern from the given alternatives.

6. What will be the order of the occurrence of the following days?
   1. Christmas   2. Independence Day
   3. Republic Day   4. Gandhi Jayanti
   (a) 4132   (b) 3241   (c) 2413   (d) 1342

7. Klien walks towards East and then towards South. After walking some distance, he turns towards West and then turns to his left. In which direction, is he walking now?
   (a) North   (b) South   (c) East   (d) West

8. The given figures in the first pair bear the certain relationship with each other, similarly in the second pair the figures must bear the same relationship. Find the missing figure in the second pair, so that they also follow the same relationship.

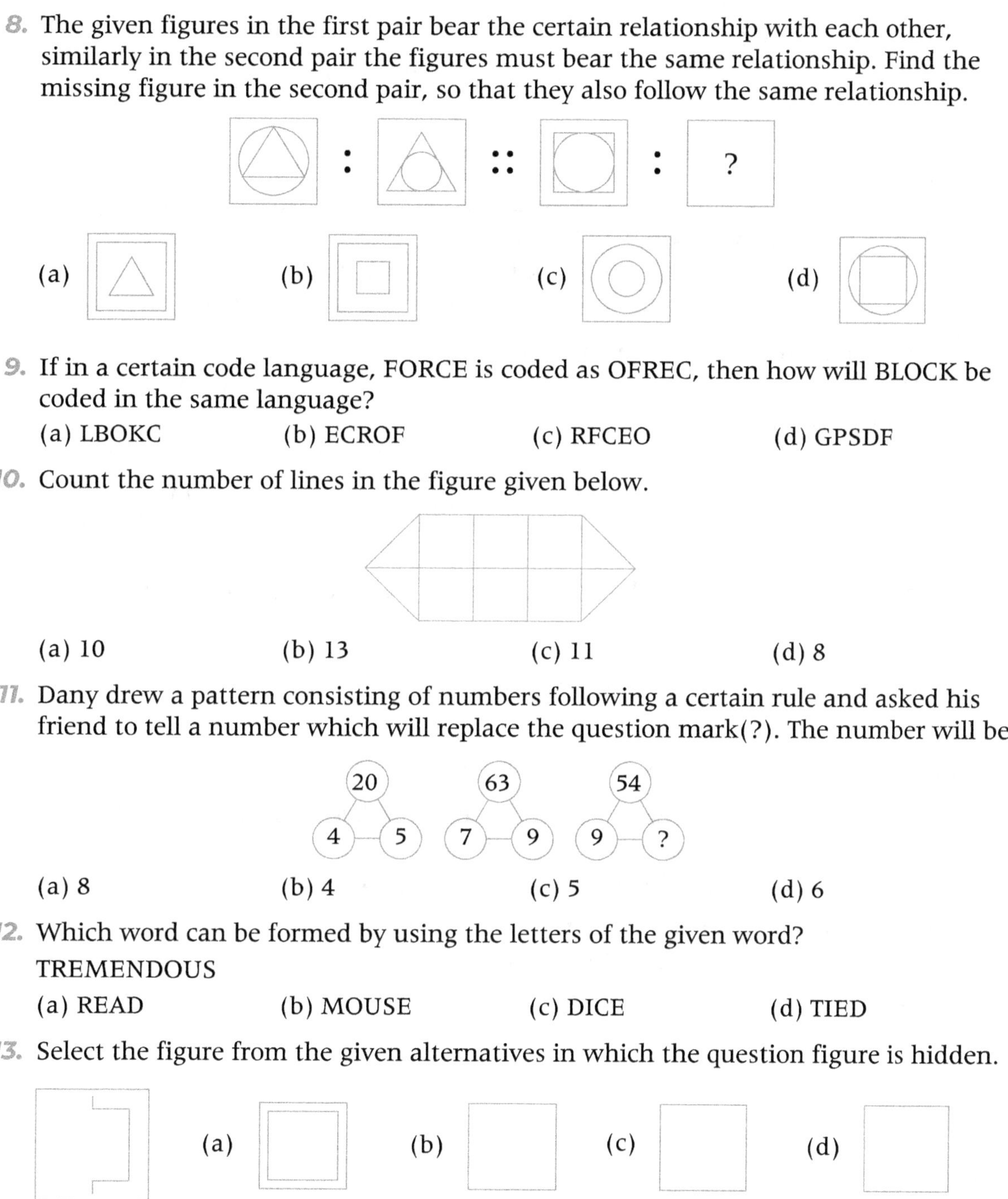

9. If in a certain code language, FORCE is coded as OFREC, then how will BLOCK be coded in the same language?

    (a) LBOKC   (b) ECROF   (c) RFCEO   (d) GPSDF

10. Count the number of lines in the figure given below.

    (a) 10   (b) 13   (c) 11   (d) 8

11. Dany drew a pattern consisting of numbers following a certain rule and asked his friend to tell a number which will replace the question mark(?). The number will be

    (a) 8   (b) 4   (c) 5   (d) 6

12. Which word can be formed by using the letters of the given word?
    TREMENDOUS

    (a) READ   (b) MOUSE   (c) DICE   (d) TIED

13. Select the figure from the given alternatives in which the question figure is hidden.

    (a)   (b)   (c)   (d)

14. Find the mirror image of the given figure

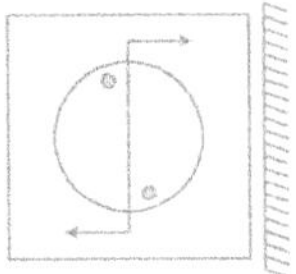

(a) 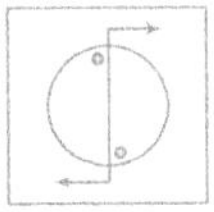   (b) 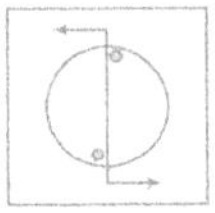   (c) 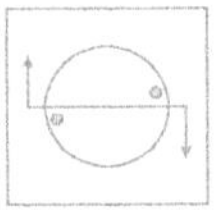   (d)

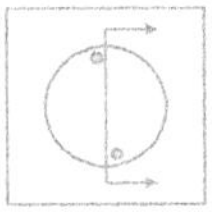

15. How many meaningful words can be formed using first, third, fifth and eighth letters from the given sequence of letters?

A C R X D V O E G L P M

(a) 1   (b) 0   (c) 3   (d) 2

16. PM is related to SJ, in the same way as GV is related to

(a) UP   (b) JS   (c) WR   (d) RU

17. Which figure is different from the others?

(a) 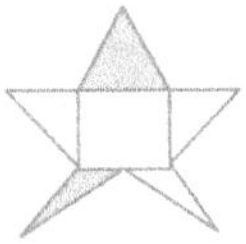   (b) 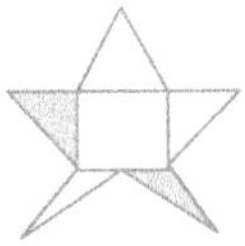   (c) 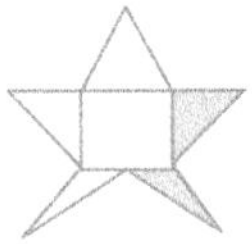   (d)

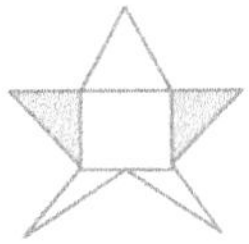

18. What number will the next bogie have, if they are following certain pattern?

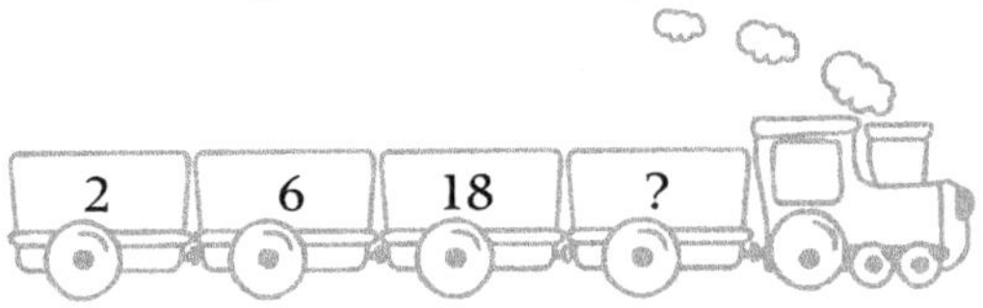

| 2 | 6 | 18 | ? |

(a) 54   (b) 60   (c) 69   (d) 36

19. If boat is called stone, stone is called tree, tree is called bat, bat is called butter and butter is called scooter, then where do the birds live?

(a) Boat   (b) Scooter   (c) Butter   (d) Bat

20. The given question is based on the following alphabet sequence

A B C D E F G H I J K L M N O P Q R S T U V W X Y Z

Which letter will be eighth from the right end?

(a) H   (b) S   (c) I   (d) T

21. Find the figure which will complete the given pattern.

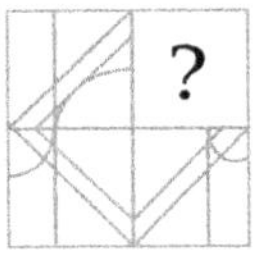

?   (a) 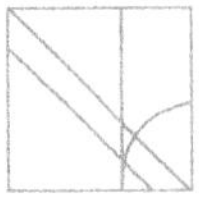   (b) 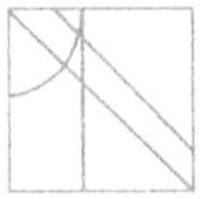   (c) 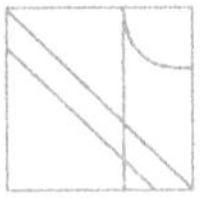   (d)

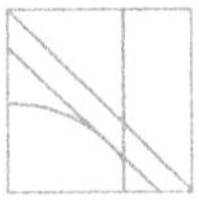

22. Identify the part of the figure which is not embedded in the question figure.

(a)   (b)   (c)   (d)

23. How many squares are there in the figure?

(a) 6   (b) 8   (c) 10   (d) 12

24. Find the mirror image of the given word.

P O G O

(a) ᗺ O G O   (b) O ᗡ O ꟼ   (c) P O ᗡ O   (d) O ᗡ O P

25. Sheela is playing with her brother and observes some numbers on certain pattern. What will be the missing number ?

```
        6  12
    ?        18
    42       24
      36  30
```

(a) 48   (b) 216   (c) 60   (d) 96

26. Some girls were standing in a line waiting for the trial of their clothes outside the fitting room of XYZ mall.

There are 3 girls ahead of Jiya and 4 girls behind her. What was the Jiya's rank from the start?

(a) 6th   (b) 3rd   (c) 4th   (d) 5th

27. The time 8 : 20 is shown in the clock below. In which direction is the minute hand face?

(a) North-East   (b) North-West   (c) South-East   (d) South-West

28. Sneha went to Delhi in January 20XX. She visited India Gate four day before fourth Saturday of January 20XX. The date on which Sneha visited India Gate

January

Sun	Mon	Tue	Wed	Thu	Fri	Sat
				1	2	3
4	5	6	7	8	9	10
11	12	13	14	15	16	17
18	19	20	21	22	23	24
25	26	27	28	29	30	31

(a) 20th January   (b) 22nd January   (c) 21st January   (d) 19th January

29. Some numbers are written on the butterflies and they are related to each other in a certain way. Find the number which will be on the last butterfly following the same patterns as the first two follow.

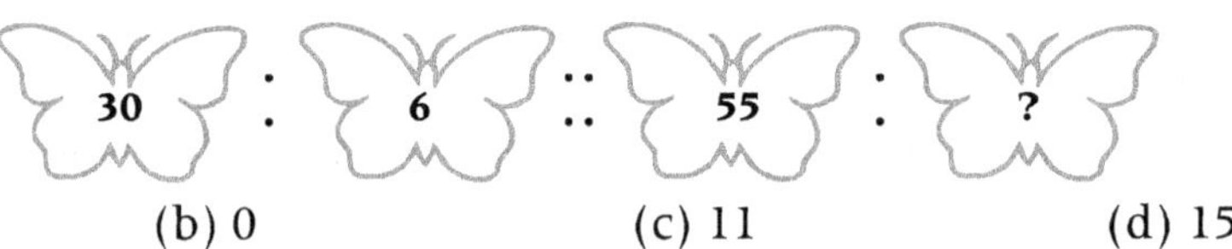

(a) 10   (b) 0   (c) 11   (d) 15

30. Observe the pattern in first three group and calculate the numbers of girls and boys in the fourth group.

(a) 4 boys 3 girls   (b) 5 girls 1 boy   (c) 4 girls 2 boys   (d) 4 girls 4 boys

Direction (Q. No. 31) Study the table and answer the questions based on it.

Letters	M	C	B	A	D	T
Codes	t	y	p	e	z	o

31. What is the code for word 'MAT'?

(a) tpz   (b) tyo   (c) teo   (d) tze

32. Find the number which is different from others in the given star?

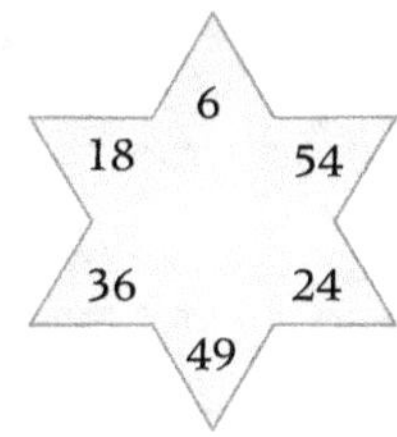

(a) 6   (b) 49   (c) 24   (d) 18

33. Adler drew following patterns for the tiles of his study room. What will be the pattern of the tile in the last block?

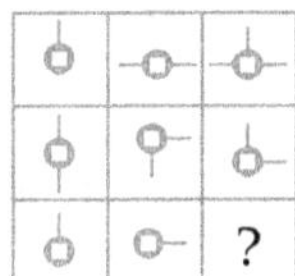 (a) 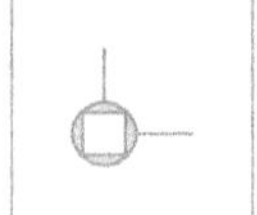 (b) 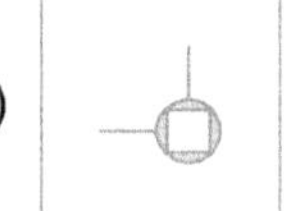 (c) 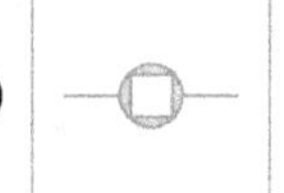 (d) 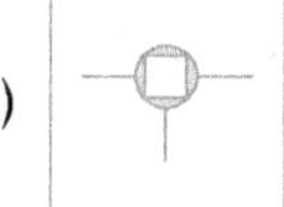

34. Some apples are arranged in a queue with colourful basket-Red colour basket-apple is 9th from the left end and 15th from the right end?

(a) 21   (b) 22   (c) 23   (d) 24

35. Four friends are getting some marks in the English class test. Siya gets more marks than Maya, Nikh gets more marks than Kinza. Kinza, gets more marks than Siya. Who among the following gets highest rank?

(a) Nikh   (b) Kinza   (c) Siya   (d) Maya

PRACTICE SET 

1. Jolly picked up four tambola coins and the numbers on them were 12, 23, 46, 72. Find an odd number from amongst them.
   (a) 12   (b) 46   (c) 23   (d) 72

2. Mango is to fruit as .... is to monument.
   (a) Tomb   (b) Red Fort   (c) Pillars   (d) History

3. Choose the combination of numbers so that letters arranged accordingly form a meaningful word.

   R T U G I A
   1 2 3 4 5 6

   (a) 542316   (b) 254312   (c) 354162   (d) 435261

4. In a certain code bucket is called basket, basket is called glass, glass is called spoon, then where are the fruits kept?
   (a) bucket   (b) glass   (c) spoon   (d) basket

5. Which figure will continue the given series?

   (a)   (b)   (c)   (d)

6. Which letter should be replaced with question mark (?) to form two meaningful words?

D			
U			
L			
?	A	T	E

   (a) L   (b) R   (c) I   (d) P

7. Arrange the given words as per their order in dictionary.
   1. Light   2. Bargain   3. Load   4. Bundle
   (a) 1423   (b) 4123   (c) 3142   (d) 2413

8. In a row of 20 students, Elina is sitting 8th from the right end and Jackie is sitting 4th from the left end, then how many students are sitting between Elina and Jackie?
   (a) 9   (b) 8   (c) 7   (d) 10

9. Which figure from the given alternatives will complete the pattern shown below?

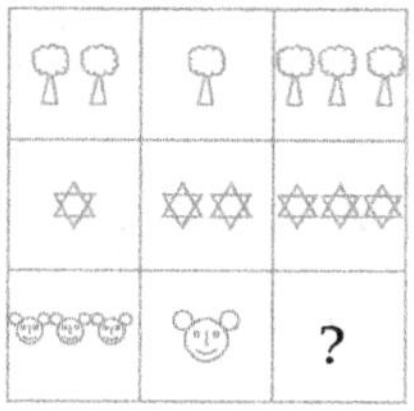

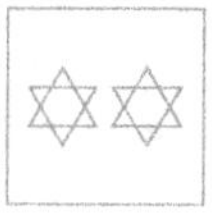

10. A policeman goes straight towards North from the police station to catch the thief, he turns to his left, then turns left again and then turns to his right. Now, in which direction is he facing?
   (a) East   (b) North   (c) South   (d) West

11. Julia drew the following figure and asked her sister to count the number of squares in that figure. The number of squares is

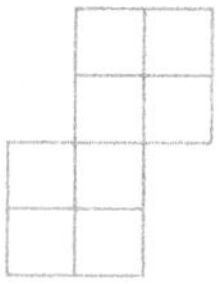

   (a) 12   (b) 13   (c) 10   (d) 14

12. Find the missing number in the given figures.

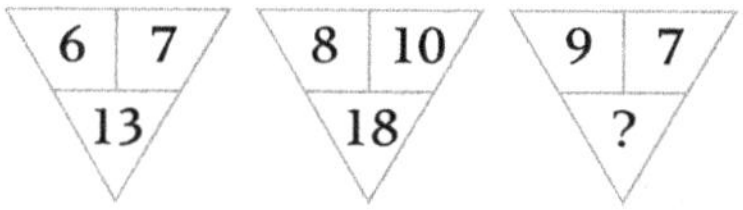

   (a) 16   (b) 15   (c) 17   (d) 20

13. Which of the following answer figures is embedded in the question figure?
   Question figure   **Answer figure**

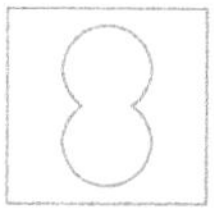

14. Choose the word from the given alternatives which cannot be formed using the letters of the given word.

DIFFERENT

(a) DIRT　　　　(b) DENT　　　　(c) TENT　　　　(d) RENT

15. Find the mirror image of the figure given below.

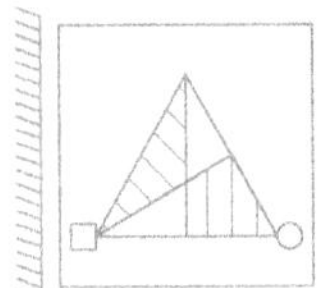　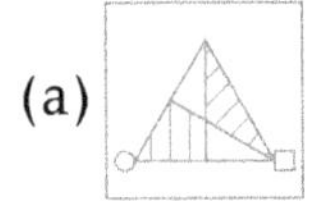 (a)　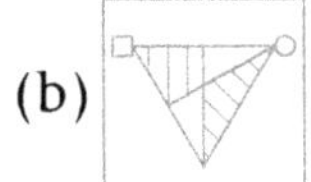 (b)　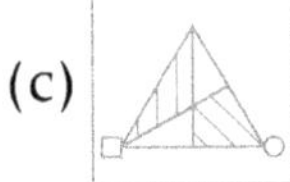 (c)　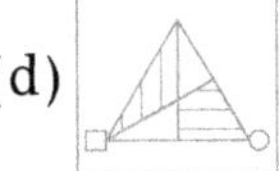 (d)

16. Some letters are written on a bottle on both sides. They are related to each other in a certain way. Find the letters that will be related to the letters on the other bottle in the same way as the first two are related.

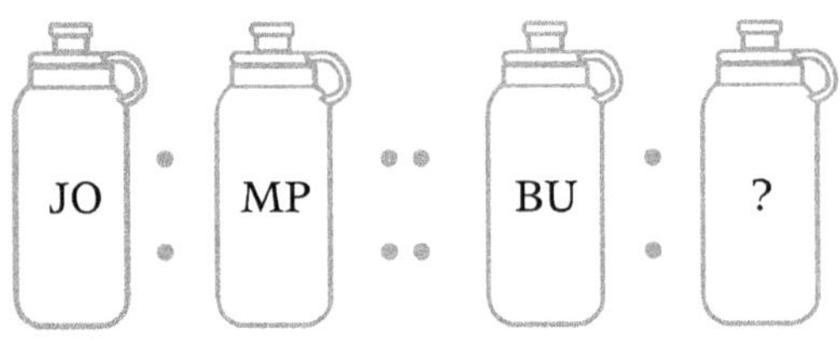

(a) VE　　　　(b) FU　　　　(c) EV　　　　(d) GV

17. In a certain code language, ROPE is coded as '#*%$' and DEAN is coded as &$@¥ then how will PEAR is coded as in the same language?

(a) %@¥#　　　　(b) %$@#　　　　(c) @%$&　　　　(d) *%@#

18. Which letter does not fit into the group

(a) Z z　　　　(b) E e　　　　(c) C c　　　　(d) P p

19. In the following figures, a pattern is followed. Find the next figure which will continue the series.

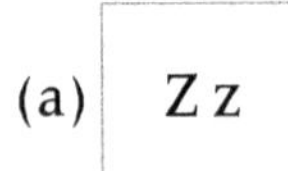　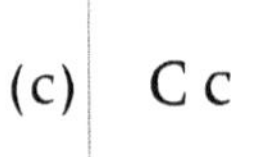　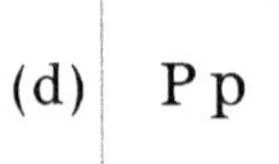　?

(a) 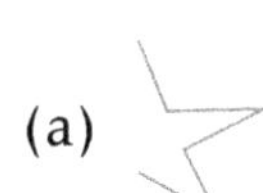　　(b) 　　(c) 　　(d) 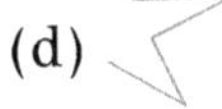

20. Find the category of given word so formed when the letters are arranged.

A R J B I N L

(a) Cloth   (b) Fruit   (c) Vegetable   (d) Colour

21. Find the figure from the alternative which will complete the given parttern.

(a)   (b)   (c)   (d)

22. What number will be displayed by last computer?

471   582   693   ?

(a) 7821   (b) 7104   (c) 784   (d) 582

23. If TESTER is coded as SETRET, then how MASTER will be coded in the same language.

(a) SAMRTE   (b) AMSRTE   (c) SAMRET   (d) RSAMET

24. Choose the word which cannot be formed using the given word.

REMEMBRANCE

(a) NUMBER   (b) MEMBER   (c) REMEMBER   (d) EMBRACE

25. Find the missing letter to complete the given matrix.

X	I	M
Y	?	N
Z	K	O

(a) L   (b) Z   (c) J   (d) P

26. Suhani drew the mirror image of her doll as shown in figure (X).

(X)

From the given options, which is the mirror image of suhani's doll?

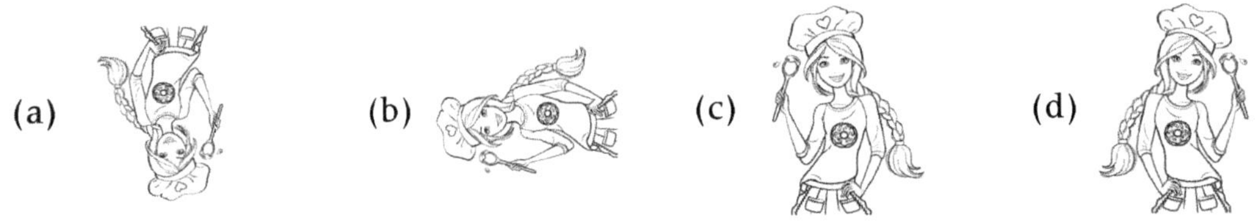

27. Rachna walks a distance of 3 km towards North, then turn her left and walk for 2 km. She again turn left and walk 3 km. How many kilometers is she from the starting point?

    (a) 4 km   (b) 3 km   (c) 6 km   (d) 2 km

28. Find the number of circles in the figure given below.

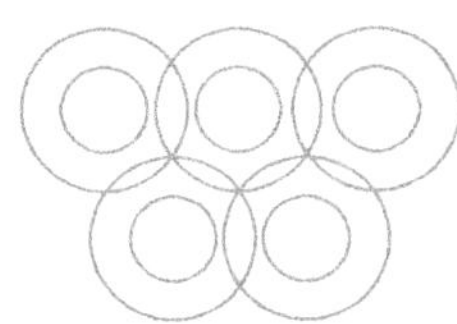

    (a) 8   (b) 9   (c) 10   (d) 11

29. Find the number which will replace the question mark (?).

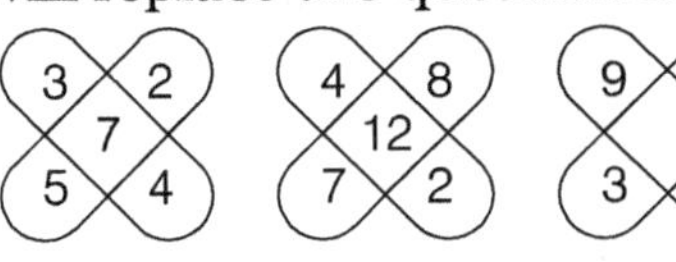

    (a) 12   (b) 10   (c) 7   (d) 11

30. Eight students went to science museum with their teacher, while entering the museum, they were in a queue as shown below.

    If Laura and Suzi interchange their positions. How many students are there between Laura and Ezak

    (a) 2   (b) 3   (c) 4   (d) 5

31. Sohan remembers that his mother's birthday is after fifteenth but before eighteenth of April whereas his sister Rakhi remembers that her mother's birthday is after sixteenth but before nineteenth of April. On which day in April is Sohan's mother's birthday?
    (a) 16th   (b) 17th   (c) 18th   (d) 19th

32. Which flower is different from amongst the following?

(a) 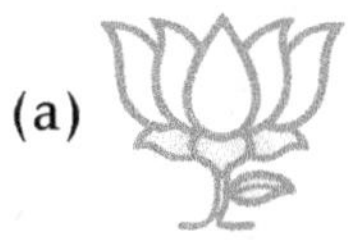   (b)    (c)    (d) 

33. Rohan and Richa are taking part in a cooking competition. Which was held three day after 2nd Sunday of February 2021. The date on which the cooking competition held?

February 2021						
Sun	Mon	Tue	Wed	Thu	Fri	Sat
	1	2	3	4	5	6
7	8	9	10	11	12	13
14	15	16	17	18	19	20
21	22	23	24	25	26	27
28						

(a) 20th February   (b) 17th February   (c) 11th February   (d) 18th February

34. What will be the mirror image of the wall clock when the mirror is on the right side

   (a) 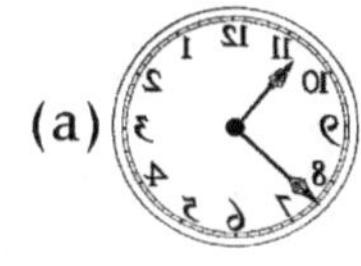   (b)    (c) 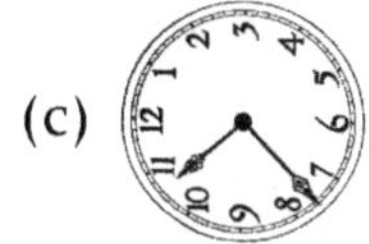   (d) 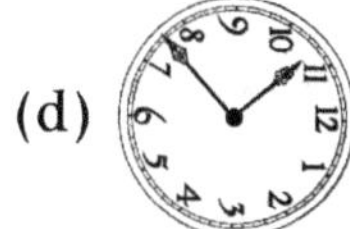

35. Jiya is facing South-East when she turns 3 right angles anti-clockwise in which place does she face now?

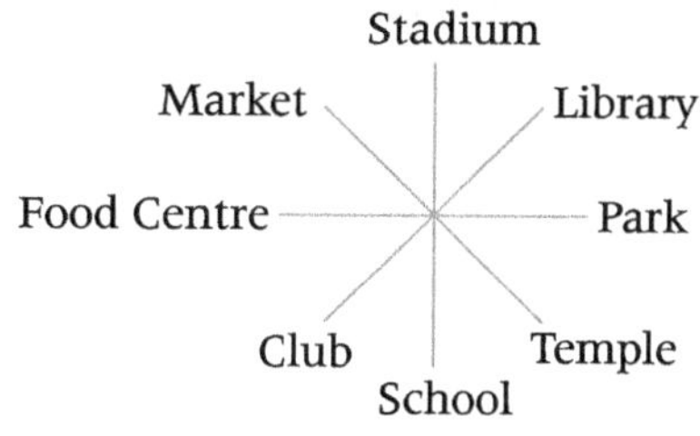

(a) Park   (b) Stadium   (c) Club   (d) Food centre

ANSWERS

1. Matching Pairs

1. (c)	2. (c)	3. (c)	4. (b)	5. (c)	6. (d)	7. (b)	8. (a)	9. (c)	10. (a)
11. (c)	12. (a)	13. (b)	14. (a)	15. (a)	16. (d)	17. (b)	18. (c)	19. (d)	20. (d)

2. Odd One Out

1. (a)	2. (b)	3. (d)	4. (c)	5. (d)	6. (d)	7. (c)	8. (a)	9. (b)	10. (a)
11. (c)	12. (d)	13. (a)	14. (d)	15. (c)	16. (d)	17. (b)	18. (d)	19. (c)	20. (d)
21. (c)	22. (c)	23. (b)							

3. What Comes Next?

1. (a)	2. (a)	3. (c)	4. (b)	5. (c)	6. (a)	7. (c)	8. (d)	9. (b)	10. (c)
11. (d)	12. (c)	13. (c)	14. (a)	15. (b)	16. (d)	17. (a)	18. (c)	19. (c)	20. (a)
21. (b)	22. (d)	23. (a)	24. (c)	25. (b)					

4. Coding-Decoding

1. (d)	2. (c)	3. (c)	4. (c)	5. (c)	6. (a)	7. (d)	8. (d)	9. (a)	10. (b)
11. (a)	12. (b)	13. (a)	14. (c)	15. (b)	16. (c)	17. (b)	18. (d)	19. (c)	20. (a)
21. (d)	22. (b)	23. (d)	24. (b)	25. (a)					

5. Alphabet and Word Formation Test

1. (d)	2. (b)	3. (a)	4. (b)	5. (a)	6. (a)	7. (b)	8. (d)	9. (d)	10. (b)
11. (d)	12. (c)	13. (a)	14. (d)	15. (c)	16. (b)	17. (b)	18. (a)	19. (c)	20. (d)

6. Complete the Figure

1. (d)	2. (b)	3. (c)	4. (a)	5. (b)	6. (a)	7. (c)	8. (c)	9. (b)	10. (c)
11. (b)	12. (c)	13. (a)	14. (c)	15. (c)	16. (c)	17. (d)	18. (b)	19. (c)	20. (c)

7. Hidden Figures

1. (a)	2. (d)	3. (a)	4. (c)	5. (c)	6. (c)	7. (b)	8. (c)	9. (c)	10. (d)
11. (a)	12. (a)	13. (a)	14. (a)	15. (c)	16. (c)	17. (d)	18. (b)	19. (d)	20. (a)

8. Counting of Figures

1. (a)	2. (b)	3. (b)	4. (c)	5. (a)	6. (c)	7. (c)	8. (a)	9. (a)	10. (d)
11. (b)	12. (d)	13. (b)	14. (d)	15. (c)					

9. Mirror Images

1. (c)	2. (b)	3. (a)	4. (c)	5. (a)	6. (b)	7. (c)	8. (d)	9. (d)	10. (d)
11. (b)	12. (b)	13. (d)	14. (b)	15. (d)	16. (d)	17. (b)	18. (a)	19. (b)	20. (b)

10. Inserting the Missing Character

1. (d)	2. (c)	3. (a)	4. (b)	5. (a)	6. (c)	7. (d)	8. (b)	9. (b)	10. (c)
11. (c)	12. (a)	13. (a)	14. (b)	15. (a)					

11. Position and Comparison Test

1. (c)	2. (d)	3. (b)	4. (b)	5. (d)	6. (c)	7. (c)	8. (a)	9. (a)	10. (a)
11. (a)	12. (a)	13. (a)	14. (d)	15. (d)					

12. Find Direction

1. (d)	2. (a)	3. (a)	4. (c)	5. (d)	6. (d)	7. (c)	8. (c)	9. (b)	10. (d)
11. (d)	12. (a)	13. (a)	14. (b)	15. (b)	16. (a)	17. (b)	18. (a)	19. (c)	20. (d)

13. Calendar Knowledge

1. (c)	2. (d)	3. (b)	4. (b)	5. (d)	6. (c)	7. (c)	8. (a)	9. (a)	10. (a)
11. (a)	12. (a)	13. (a)	14. (d)	15. (d)					

Practice Set 1

1. (b)	2. (b)	3. (d)	4. (c)	5. (a)	6. (b)	7. (b)	8. (d)	9. (a)	10. (c)
11. (d)	12 (b)	13. (c)	14. (b)	15. (c)	16. (b)	17. (c)	18. (a)	19. (d)	20. (b)
21. (d)	22. (c)	23. (a)	24. (b)	25. (a)	26. (d)	27. (c)	28. (a)	29 (c)	30. (d)
31. (c)	32. (b)	33. (a)	34. (c)	35. (a)					

Practice Set 2

1. (c)	2. (b)	3. (d)	4. (b)	5. (c)	6. (a)	7. (d)	8. (b)	9. (d)	10. (d)
11. (c)	12 (a)	13. (d)	14. (c)	15. (a)	16. (c)	17. (b)	18. (b)	19. (c)	20. (c)
21. (b)	22. (b)	23. (c)	24. (a)	25. (c)	26. (d)	27. (d)	28. (c)	29 (b)	30. (c)
31. (b)	32. (d)	33. (b)	34. (a)	35 (c)					

Hints & Solutions

1. Matching Pairs

1. (*c*) The first figure in the first pair gets inverted to obtain the second figure. Similarly, the first figure in the second pair must be inverted to obtain the missing figure.

2. (*c*) As, in the first pair, circles are inserted inside the triangle. Similarly, the circles must also be inserted in the square as shown in option figure (c). Hence, option (c) is correct.

3. (*c*) Figure (i) and (iii) are formed by curved lines and figure (ii) and (iv) are formed by only straight lines. So, option (c) will complete the given set of pattern. Hence, option (c) is correct.

4. (*b*) Figure (iii) is the mirror image of figure (i). In the same way figure (ii) will be related to figure (iv). Hence, option (b) is correct.

5. (*c*) As, $11 \xrightarrow{\times 2} 22$ Similarly, $12 \xrightarrow{\times 2} \boxed{24}$

6. (*d*) As, $3 \times 3 \times 3 = 27$ Similarly, $5 \times 5 \times 5 = \boxed{125}$

7. (*b*) As, $25 \xrightarrow{\div 5} 5$ Similarly, $40 \xrightarrow{\div 5} \boxed{8}$

8. (*a*) As, $49 = 7 \times 7$ Similarly, $121 = 11 \times 11$
So, 11 number on the last ticket.

9. (*c*) As, $3\,\widehat{(8)}\,9 \;:\; 8$ Similarly, $4\,\widehat{(6)}\,2 \;:\; \boxed{6}$

10. (*a*) As, $\begin{array}{cc} \text{B} & \text{A} \\ {\scriptstyle +4}\downarrow & {\scriptstyle +4}\downarrow \\ \text{F} & \text{E} \end{array}$ Similarly, $\begin{array}{cc} \text{L} & \text{K} \\ {\scriptstyle +4}\downarrow & {\scriptstyle +4}\downarrow \\ \boxed{\text{P} \;\; \text{O}} \end{array}$

11. (*c*) As, $\begin{array}{ccc} \text{X} & \text{T} & \text{V} \\ {\scriptstyle -3}\downarrow & {\scriptstyle -3}\downarrow & {\scriptstyle -3}\downarrow \\ \text{U} & \text{Q} & \text{S} \end{array}$

Similarly, $\begin{array}{ccc} \text{P} & \text{M} & \text{Q} \\ {\scriptstyle -3}\downarrow & {\scriptstyle -3}\downarrow & {\scriptstyle -3}\downarrow \\ \boxed{\text{M} \;\; \text{J} \;\; \text{N}} \end{array}$

12. (*a*) Warrior uses the sword to fight in the war. Similarly, writer uses the pen to write with.

13. (*b*) As, coffee is obtained from seeds. Similarly, tea is obtained from leaves.

14. (*a*) As, $\begin{array}{l} \text{K} \xrightarrow{+3} \text{N} \\ \text{T} \xrightarrow{-2} \text{R} \\ \text{M} \xrightarrow{+1} \text{N} \end{array}$ Similarly, $\boxed{\begin{array}{l} \text{I} \xrightarrow{+3} \text{L} \\ \text{R} \xrightarrow{-2} \text{P} \\ \text{V} \xrightarrow{+1} \text{W} \end{array}}$

15. (*a*) As, $\begin{array}{cc} \text{F} & \text{H} \\ {\scriptstyle -2}\downarrow & {\scriptstyle -2}\downarrow \\ \text{D} & \text{F} \end{array}$ Similarly, $\begin{array}{cc} \text{U} & \text{Y} \\ {\scriptstyle -2}\downarrow & {\scriptstyle -2}\downarrow \\ \boxed{\text{S} \;\; \text{W}} \end{array}$

16. (*d*) As, $\begin{array}{ccc} \text{A} & \text{B} & \text{C} \\ & \times & \\ \text{C} & \text{B} & \text{A} \end{array}$

Similarly, $\begin{array}{ccc} \text{Q} & \text{M} & \text{P} \\ & \times & \\ \boxed{\text{P} \;\; \text{M} \;\; \text{Q}} \end{array}$

17. (*b*) Letter 'H' is added at the starting of the word 'Eat' to get the word 'Heat'. Similarly, 'H' is to be added in the word 'Arm' to get the word 'Harm'.

18. (*c*) As, pear is a fruit. Similarly, spinach is a vegetable.

19. (*d*) As, we do exercise in gym. Similarly, we eat food in restaurant.

20. (*d*) As, 'LION' has 4 letters, similarly, 'TIGER' has 5 letters.
Thus, option (d) is correct.

21. (*c*) As, India has 5 letters.
So, $5^2 = 25$
'NAGALAND' has 8 letters.
So, $8^2 = 64$
Hence, option (c) is correct.

22. (*b*) Here, in the given word, every letter has been given in its alphabetical position number.

As, $\begin{array}{ccccc} \text{M} & \text{E} & \text{E} & \text{R} & \text{A} \\ \downarrow & \downarrow & \downarrow & \downarrow & \downarrow \\ 13 & 5 & 5 & 18 & 1 \end{array}$

Similarly, $\begin{array}{cccccc} \text{M} & \text{A} & \text{D} & \text{H} & \text{A} & \text{V} \\ \downarrow & \downarrow & \downarrow & \downarrow & \downarrow & \downarrow \\ \boxed{13 \;\; 1 \;\; 4 \;\; 8 \;\; 1 \;\; 22} \end{array}$

2. Odd One Out

1. (a) In all the caps except option (a), a ball is hanging at the top, while in option (a), a square like shape is hanging.

2. (b) In all the pictures except option (b), the lower part is shaded, whereas in option (b), the upper part is shaded.

3. (d) In all the figures except option (d), the arrows are pointing outward, while in option (d), they are pointing inward.

4. (c) In all the figures except option (c), the eyes are in the same direction.

5. (d) Except option (d) all are basic needs of school, a bag, lunch-box and book.

   Hence, option (d) is correct.

6. (d) In option (a), (b), (c) the number of sides of outer figure is one more than the sides of inner figure while option (d) inner figure has no side.

   Hence, option (d) is correct.

7. (c) In all the figures except option (c), the shaded portion is carried forward.

8. (a) All except the number on the ball, '19' is not divisible by '3'.

   So, '19' is odd one out.

9. (b) Only the number in option (b), is divisible by '2'. So, 32 is different.

10. (a) Except (a) all other numbers are divisible by 4.

11. (c) Number inside the shapes is the square of the sides of the figure.

    Hence, option (c) is correct.

12. (d) All except '345', is the even number.

    So, 345 is different from others.

13. (a) All the letters except 'T', are made with the combination of straight and curved lines.

14. (d) The letters follow the below pattern

    $$B \xrightarrow{+2} D, \ C \xrightarrow{+2} E,$$
    $$F \xrightarrow{+2} H, N \xrightarrow{-2} L,$$

    Except NL, all others follow same pattern.

15. (c) The letters in the pair make a sum of 27.

    B = Y (Reverser letter)

    I = R (Reverse letter)

N = P (Reverse letter of N is M not P)

L = O (Reverse letter)

So, NP is different.

16. (d) $$J \xrightarrow{+1} K \xrightarrow{+1} L,$$
    $$G \xrightarrow{+1} H \xrightarrow{+1} I$$
    $$O \xrightarrow{+1} P \xrightarrow{+1} Q$$
    $$\text{and} \ \ I \xrightarrow{+3} L \xrightarrow{+8} T$$

    Except ILT, all others follow same pattern.

17. (b) Except option (b), there is no repetition of any letter in any other group.

    Hence, option (b) is correct.

18. (d) This is the only group containing two small letters.

    Hence, option (d) is correct.

19. (c) The noun, preposition, and adverb are parts of speech but punctuation is not a parts of speech.

    Hence, option (c) is correct.

20. (d) Except piano, all are string based instruments.

    So, piano is different.

21. (c) Except June, all the given months have 31 days. While June has 30 days.

    So, June is different.

22. (c) Except sugar, all other are spices.

    So, sugar is odd one.

23. (b) The student would have picked out bone. Except bone, all others are external body parts, whereas bone is an internal body part.

    So, bone is different.

24. (d) In all pairs except (d), first is used to contain the second.

25. (b) In all others, second denotes the class to which the first belongs.

3. What Comes Next?

1. (a) Here, one leaf is removed alternatively, first from right and then from left. Now, there will be three leaves in the last part which is given in option (a).

2. (a) Here, in every next step, an element is added. In first step, an arc is added. In second step, a line is added, now in third step a small circle at the top is to be added.

3. (*c*) In the given set of figures, a line and a circle is added in every step to get the next figure. So, the figure in option (c) will replace the question mark.

4. (*b*) Alternate, arrows are same. So, the arrows in the fifth figure will be same as the arrows in the first and third figure. Thus, option figure (b) will continue the series.

5. (*c*) Alternatively, one line is added in the lower part and the upper part. Now, the line should be added in the upper part.

   So, the next figure will have two lines in the upper as well as in the lower part.

6. (*a*) In the series of figures, the arrow rotates one- eight in clockwise direction (to the right) and the shaded portion also move from one corner to the next in the clockwise direction (to the right). So, figure in option (a) will be the exact position of the figure.

7. (*c*) From the first figure, a line is removed to get the second figure, similarly a line is removed from the second figure in clockwise direction to get the next figure.

   On following this pattern, option figure (c) will continue the series.

8. (*d*) First figure is like the fourth figure only the circle in the centre is white and the curve at the top is in the opposite direction in the fourth figure. So, the figure that will come next in the sequence will be like the third figure following the same changes as given in option (d).

9. (*b*) From the first figure, side and a line on top are added to get the next figure.

   So, the fourth figure will have six sides and six lines on the top as in option (b).

10. (*c*) Here in every step, square with a star is static and the triangle with a star rotate $180°$ in each step in forward direction, so, the next figure will be option (c) figure.

    Hence, option (c) is correct.

11. (*d*) Given pattern follow a rule as pattern 1 having 4 Boxes. Pattern 2 having $4 \times 2 = 8$ Boxes and Pattern 3 having 4×3 i.e. 12 Boxes and so on. In same way 10th pattern will have 4×10 i.e. 40 boxes.

12. (*c*) The pattern is as follows:
$$1 \times 1 = 1, 2 \times 2 = 4 = 3 \times 3 = \boxed{9}$$

$$4 \times 4 = 16, 5 \times 5 = 25$$

The natural numbers from 1 to 5 are multiplied with themselves.

So, '9' will replace the question mark.

13. (*c*) The pattern is as follows:
$$4 + 4 = 8, \quad 8 + 4 = \boxed{12},$$
$$12 + 4 = 16$$

So, the missing card number is '12'.

14. (*a*) The pattern is as follows :
$$20 - 1 = 19, \quad 19 - 2 = 17,$$
$$17 - 3 = \boxed{14}$$

So, the last bag number will be '14'.

15. (*b*) The pattern is as follows:
$$5 + 1 = 6, 6 + 2 = 8,$$
$$8 + 3 = 11$$

So, '11' will be the next t-shirt number.

16. (*d*) The bells follow the sequence as
$$2 \xrightarrow{+1} 3 \xrightarrow{+1} \boxed{4} \xrightarrow{+1} 5$$
$$8 \xrightarrow{-1} 7 \xrightarrow{-1} \boxed{6} \xrightarrow{-1} 5$$
$$3 \xrightarrow{+1} 4 \xrightarrow{+1} \boxed{5} \xrightarrow{+1} 6$$

So, '465' will be depicted on the third bell.

17. (*a*) The pattern is as follows :
$$7 \xrightarrow{+7} 14 \xrightarrow{+7} 21 \xrightarrow{+7} 28 \xrightarrow{+7} 35 \xrightarrow{+7} 42 \xrightarrow{+7} \boxed{49}$$

So, 49 will be displayed by last LED display.

18. (*c*) The pattern is as follows :
   As,   In sky $1 = 6 \times 1 = 6$
   In sky $2 = 6 \times 2 = 12$
   And so on ....
   Similarly, In sky $13 = 6 \times 13 = \boxed{78}$

19. (*c*) The pattern is as follows :
   4 is added in each number in forward direction.
   As, $10 + 4 = 14, 18 + 4 = 22,$
   $$22 + 4 = 26, 26 + 4 = 30$$
   Similarly, $13 + 4 = 17, 17 + 4 = 21,$
   $$21 + 4 = 25, 25 + 4 = 29, 29 + 4 = 33$$
   Hence, option (c) is correct.

20. (*a*) The pattern is as follows :
$$D \xrightarrow{+3} G \xrightarrow{+3} J \xrightarrow{+3} M \xrightarrow{+3} \boxed{P}$$
   So, 'P' will come in last diamond.

21. (*b*) The sequence is as follows
$$A \xrightarrow[\text{Opposite}]{} Z, B \xrightarrow[\text{Opposite}]{} Y, C \xrightarrow[\text{Opposite}]{} X$$

So, the next combination will be

$$D \xrightarrow{\text{Opposite}} W$$

22. (*d*) The pattern is as follows:

$$P \xrightarrow{+1} Q \xrightarrow{+1} R \xrightarrow{+1} S \xrightarrow{+1} \boxed{T}$$
$$Q \xrightarrow{+2} S \xrightarrow{+2} U \xrightarrow{+2} W \xrightarrow{+2} \boxed{Y}$$

So, 'TY' will continue the pattern.

23. (*a*) The pattern is as follows :

Ist series, $G \xrightarrow{+2} I \xrightarrow{+2} \boxed{K} \xrightarrow{+2} M \xrightarrow{+2} O \xrightarrow{+2} Q$

IInd series, $M \xrightarrow{+2} O \xrightarrow{+2} \boxed{Q} \xrightarrow{+2} S \xrightarrow{+2} U \xrightarrow{+2} W$

IIIrd series, $T \xrightarrow{+2} V \xrightarrow{+2} \boxed{X} \xrightarrow{+2} Z \xrightarrow{+2} B \xrightarrow{+2} D$

Hence, option (a) is correct.

24. (*c*) The pattern is as follows :

Ist series, $A \xrightarrow{+1} B \xrightarrow{+2} D \xrightarrow{+3} G \xrightarrow{+4} \boxed{K}$

IInd series, $D \xrightarrow{+1} E \xrightarrow{+2} G \xrightarrow{+3} J \xrightarrow{+4} \boxed{N}$

IIIrd series, $E \xrightarrow{+1} F \xrightarrow{+2} H \xrightarrow{+3} K \xrightarrow{+4} \boxed{O}$

So, the pair of letters 'KNO' come in last.

25. (*b*) The pattern is as follows

$$A \xrightarrow{+2} C \xrightarrow{+2} E \xrightarrow{+2} G \xrightarrow{+2} \boxed{I}$$
$$M \xrightarrow{+1} N \xrightarrow{+1} O \xrightarrow{+1} P \xrightarrow{+1} \boxed{Q}$$

4. Coding Decoding

1. (*d*) Since, $\triangle$ = C, $\diamond$ = R, $\oslash$ = B

and $\square$ = S

So, the code for the given figures will be 'CRBS'.

2. (c) We get fruit from 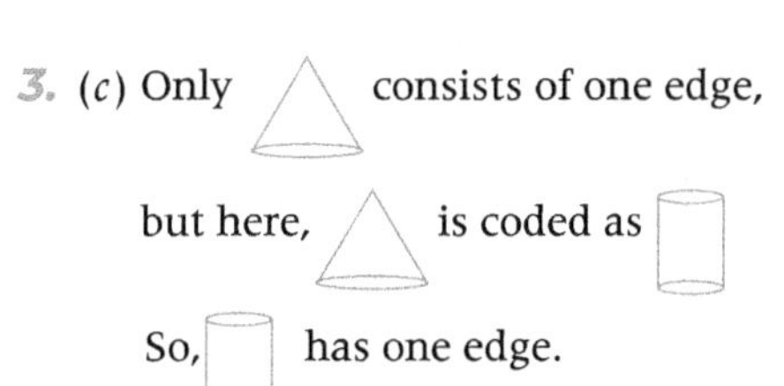 and here is called . So, we get fruit from .

3. (c) Only $\triangle$ consists of one edge,

but here, $\triangle$ is coded as $\square$

So, $\square$ has one edge.

4. (*c*) Since, J → e, A → t, C → y, K → q
So, JACK is coded as 'etyq'.

5. (*a*) As, 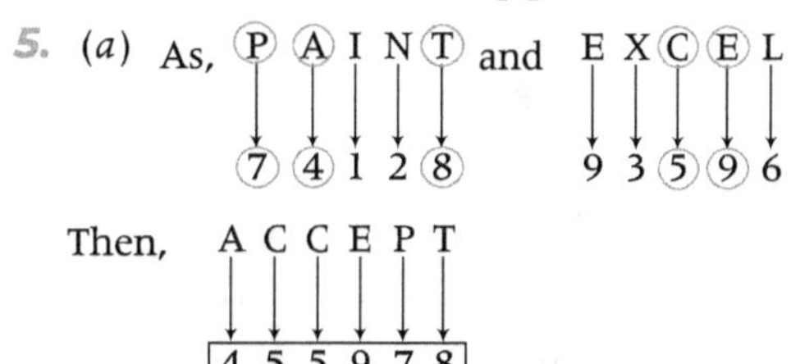

Then,
$$\begin{array}{cccccc} A & C & C & E & P & T \\ \downarrow & \downarrow & \downarrow & \downarrow & \downarrow & \downarrow \\ \end{array}$$
$$\boxed{4\ \ 5\ \ 5\ \ 9\ \ 7\ \ 8}$$

So, ACCEPT will be coded as '455978'.

6. (*d*) Since, '32' means CB according to the position of letters in the English alphabet. In the same way, '54' means 'ED'.

7. (*a*)

As, 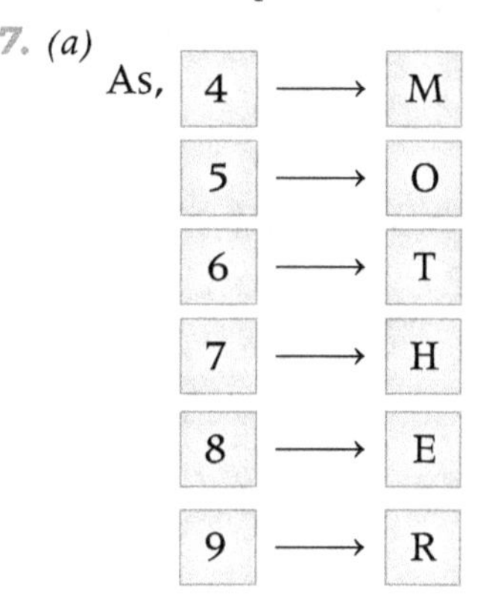

Similarly,
$$\begin{array}{cccc} 7 & 4 & 8 & 6 \\ \downarrow & \downarrow & \downarrow & \downarrow \\ \end{array}$$
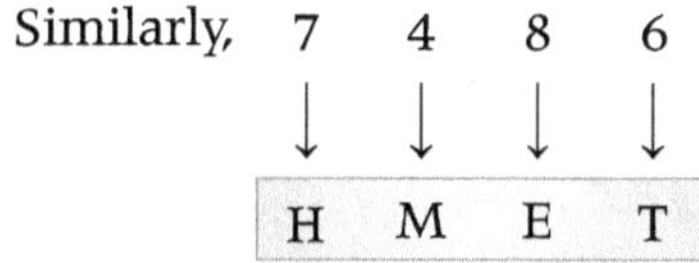

So, code for '7486' is 'HMET'.
Hence, option (a) is correct.

8. (*b*) In the first and second statement the common code is 8 and the common word is smart. Therefore, 8 means smart.

Hence, option (b) is correct.

9. (*a*) As, 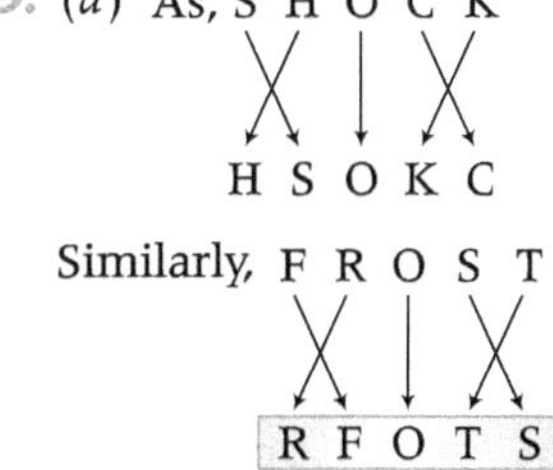

So, FROST is coded as 'RFOTS'.

10. (*b*) As, H A P P Y   Similarly, V O W E L

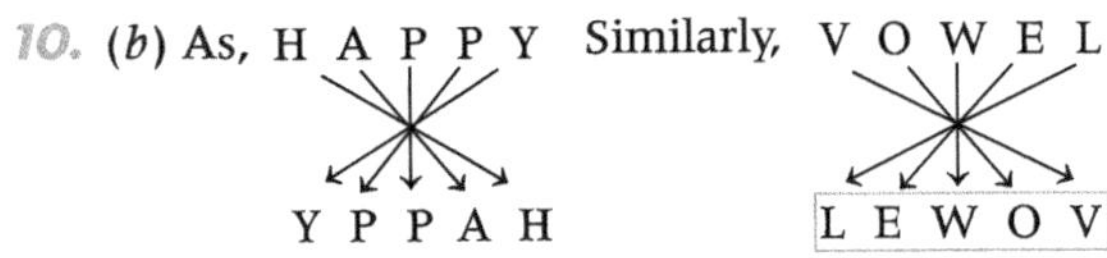

Y P P A H   L E W O V

11. (*c*) As, P L A N E T

$+1$ $+1$ $+1$ $+1$ $+1$ $+1$

Q M B O F U

Similarly, B E T T E R

$+1$ $+1$ $+1$ $+1$ $+1$ $+1$

C F U U F S

So, BETTER is coded as CFUUFS.

12. (*b*) As, S N A K E

$+2$ $+2$ $+2$ $+2$ $+2$

U P C M G

Similarly, J A P A N

$+2$ $+2$ $+2$ $+2$ $+2$

L C R C P

So, JAPAN is coded as 'LCRCP'.

13. (*c*) As, (R)A T and (C)A T Then, C A R

↓ ↓ ↓   (↓)(↓)↓   ↓ ↓ ↓

* Δ %   (#)(Δ)%   # Δ *

So, 'CAR' is coded as '#Δ*'.

14. (*b*) As, S ⟶ 5

N ⟶ @

O ⟶ g

W ⟶ #

So, SNOW will be written as 5@g#.

15. (*d*) As,

C	O	O	K	M
@	<	<	#	%

So,

C	O	O	K
@	<	@	#

Hence, option (d) is correct.

16. (*c*) Clothes are washed by soap and here soap is called ink.

So, 'ink' is used for washing clothes.

17. (*a*) A man tastes food by tongue and here tongue is called foot.

So, man tastes food with foot.

18. (*c*) We know that capital of West Bengal is Kolkata. But here Kolkata is called Gandhinagar.

19. (*b*) Since, symbol of currency of India is ₹ and here ₹ is called ¥. So, the symbol of the currency of India is ¥.

20. (*d*) In roman numerals, V comes after IV but here V means VI. So, VI comes after IV.

21. (*b*) In roman numerals, X comes immediately after IX. But here X means C. So, C will come immediate after IX.

Hence, option (b) is correct.

22. (*a*) Your answer would be follows :

Order Code	Items in Basket
1	Put 2 Mangoes
2	Put 2 Dairy milks
3	Take out 1 Mango

On observing the above table, we get

$= 2\,(\text{Mangoes}) + 2\,(\text{Dairy milks})$

$- 1\,(\text{Take out mango})$

$= 2 + 2 - 1 = 3$

Hence, '3' items would be in the basket.

5. Alphabet and Word Formation Test

1. (*d*) 'D' is the letter that will complete the first word BIR**D** and beginning the second word **D**UCK.

2. (*b*) Letter 'T' will replace the question mark and make two meaningful words MAR**T** and FOR**T**.

3. (*a*) 'E' is the letter that will complete the first word SHAP**E** and beginning the second word **E**YES.

4. (*b*) The letter 'A' must be replaced with the question mark to form two meaningful words, P**A**IR and C**A**RE.

5. (*a*) The word which can be formed is HAND and HAND is a body part.

6. (*a*) The word which can be formed by using the given letters is SHIRT and the correct sequence of numbers is '21435'.

7. (*b*) RISE is the only word which can be formed by using the letters of the word EXERCISE.

8. (*d*) The word NATION cannot be formed using the letters of the given word EDUCATION, since only single 'N' is there in the given word.

9. (*d*) The letter common in REPEAT and ARTIST is 'A' and it occurs only once in both the words. 'A' does not come in the word REPEL .

10. (*b*) The letter according to the given sequence is 'I'.

11. (*c*) If we dropped all the vowels the sequence is

LCFPKMBGDHQJRNSVXZT $\boxed{\text{Y}}$ W
                          2nd

Here, 'Y' will be 2nd from the right end.

12. (*c*) The words according to English dictionary can be arranged as shown below

Bunch→Direct→Improve→Petition
  1   4   3   2

So, the correct sequence is '1432'.

13. (*a*) The given words according to English dictionary can be arranged as shown below

Harmony →Host→Raise→Resident
   3   1   4   2

So, the correct sequence is '3142'.

14. (*d*) The given words can be arranged in meaningful order as shown below

Day→ Week→ Month→ Year
 4   1   3   2

So, the correct sequence is '4132'.

15. (*c*) The correct sequence of given words is shown below

Grass→Grasshopper→Frog→Snake
  2   4   1   3

So, the correct sequence is '2413'.

16. (*b*) The order is as follows

Elephant → Horse → Lion → Tiger
   2   1   4   3

So, the alphabetical order = 2, 1, 4, 3.

17. (*b*) The order is as follows

Chin → Head → Nose → Legs
  2   3   1   4

So, the alphabetical order = 2, 3, 1, 4

18. (*a*) (a) A   B   D   G
                 $+1$ $+2$ $+3$

(b) L   N   O   Q
     $+2$ $+1$ $+2$

(c) B   E   G   H
     $+3$ $+2$ $+1$

(d) L   N   O   R
     $+2$ $+1$ $+3$

So, series in option (a) follow the rule.

Hence, option (a) is correct.

19. (*c*) Here,

Corona + Virus = Corona Virus = 2C

20. (*d*) Here, Video + Game = Videogame = 1 Y

6. Complete the Figure

1. (*d*) Figure in option (d) will be the pattern on the fourth tile.

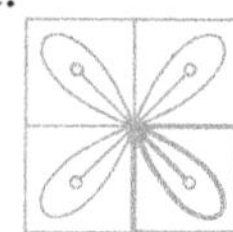

The completed pattern can be shown in above figure.

2. (*b*) Figure in option (b) will complete the given pattern.

The completed pattern can be shown in given below figure.

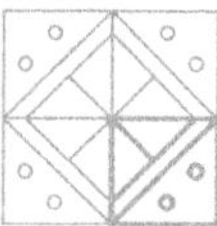

3. (*c*) The figure in option (c) will complete the given pattern.

The completed pattern can be shown in above figure.

4. *(a)* The figure in option (a) will complete the pattern.

The completed pattern can be shown in given below figure.

5. *(b)* Figure in option (b) will complete the pattern of the spider web.

The completed spider web will look like as shown below

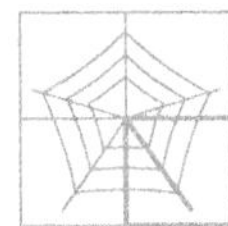

6. *(d)* Harper's missing book cover is shown in option (d). The whole cover will look like as shown below

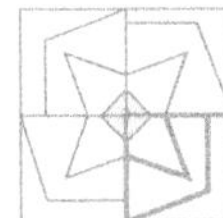

7. *(c)* In the given box in first row, second figure resembles from first. Similarly in second row, second figure resembles from figure in option (c). Hence option (c) is correct.

8. *(c)* Figure (c) will complete the pattern.

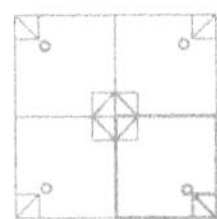

9. *(c)* On close observation, we find that the option (c) will complete the pattern when placed in the blank space of question figure as shown below

Hence, option (c) is correct.

10. *(c)* On close observation, we find that the option (c) will complete the pattern when placed in the blank space of question figure as shown below :

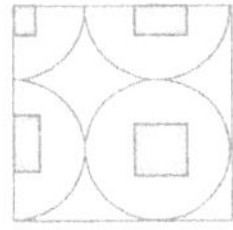

Hence, option (c) is correct.

11. *(a)* On close observation, we find that the option (a) will complete the pattern when placed in the blank space of question figure as shown below :

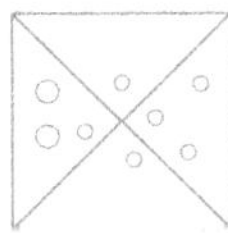

Hence, option (a) is correct.

12. *(d)* On close observation, we find that the option (d) will complete the pattern when placed in the blank space of question figure as shown below

Hence, option (d) is correct.

13. *(d)* The pattern of the fourth tile is shown in option (d) as in each row one upper and one lower part is shaded.

The pattern would appear as shown.

14. *(b)* On close observation, we find that the option (b) will complete the pattern when placed in the blank space of question figure as shown below :

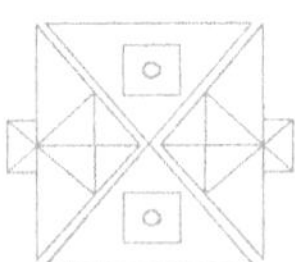

Hence, option (b) is correct.

15. *(d)* Figure in option (d) will complete the pattern as the first element is same in each row but the second element increases in number by one.

16. *(c)* The figure in option (c) will be the pattern in the last block. From second to third, the lines in between are removed.

17. (*d*) The first element of the row 1 is half shaded, the second element is $\frac{1}{4}$ th shaded and the last is blank.

Same pattern must be followed in the third row.

18. (*b*) One line is increasing in each subsequent figure.

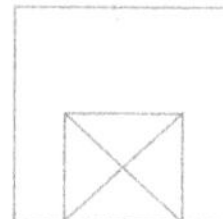

Hence, option (b) is correct.

19. (*c*) By observing the above pattern figure (c) will complete the matrix.

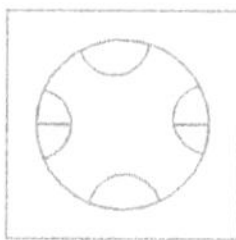

Hence, option (c) is correct.

20. (*b*) In the given matrix. In first row there are 2 lines, in second row there are 3 ovals and in third row here are 3 arrows so, figure in option (b) will complete the figure matrix.

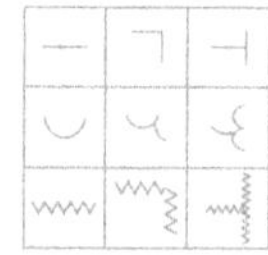

7. Hidden Figures

1. (*a*) Figure in option (a) is exactly embedded in the problem figure (X) and can be shown in figure below.

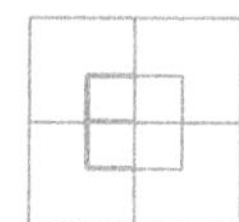

2. (*d*) Option figure (d) is hidden in the problem figure (X) and can be shown in figure below.

3. (*a*) Part given in option (a) is exactly embedded in the given figure (X) and can be shown in figure below.

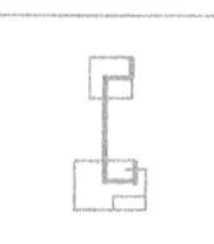

4. (*c*) Figure in option (c) is embedded in the problem figure and can be shown in figure below.

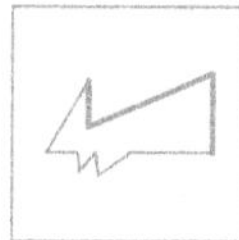

5. (*c*) Figure in option (c) is exactly hidden in the problem figure (X).
The hidden figure can be shown in figure below.

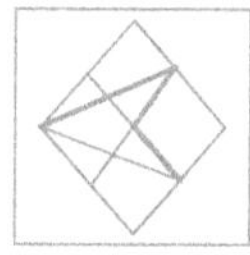

6. (*c*) Figure in option (c) is exactly embedded in the given figure (X).

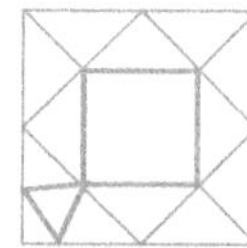

The embedded figure can be shown in figure below.

7. (*b*) Option figure (b) is hidden in problem figure (X) and can be shown in figure below.

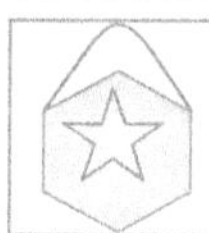

8. (*c*) Figure in option (c) is not embedded in the question figure. Whereas all the other figures are embedded.

9. (*c*) Figure in option (c) is not hidden in the question figure, whereas all the other figures are hidden.

10. (*c*) Figure in option (c) is not hidden in the question figure. Whereas, all the other figures are hidden.

11. (*a*) The given figure (X) is hidden in option (a) and can be shown in figure below .

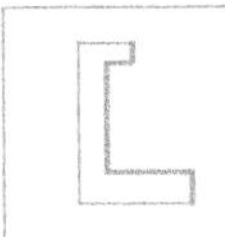

12. (*a*) In option figure (a), the given figure (X) is embedded and this can be shown in figure below.

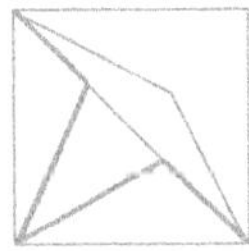

13. (*a*) The given figure (X) is exactly embedded in the option figure (a) and this can be shown in figure below.

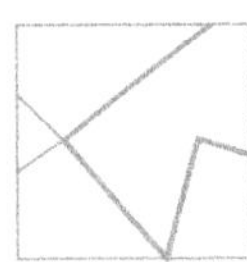

14. (*a*) The given figure (X) is embedded in option figure (a) and this can be shown in figure below.

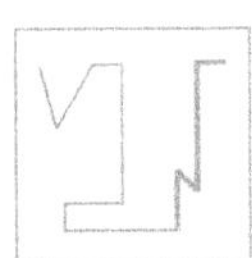

15. (*c*) Figure (X) is embedded in option figure (c) and can be shown in figure below.

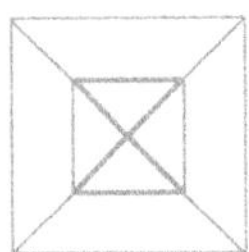

16. (*c*) The given figure (X) is embedded in option figure (c) as shown in figure below.

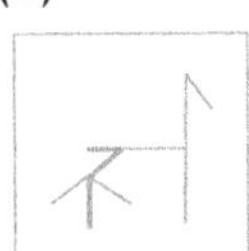

17. (*d*) The given figure (X) is embedded in option figure (d) and this can be shown in figure below.

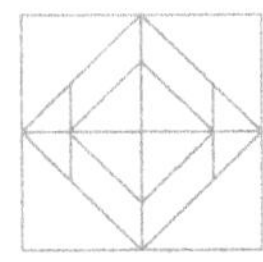

18. (b) Figure (X) is embedded in option figure (b) can be shown in figurebelow.

19. (*d*) Figure (X) is embedded in option figure (d) can be shown in figure below.

20. (a) Figure (X) is embedded in option figure (a) can be shown in figure below.

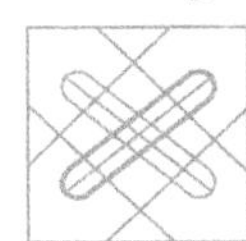

8. Counting of Figures

1. (*a*) The given figure can be labelled as shown in figure below.

7	8
1	2
3	4

Single unit rectangles $= 4$

Rectangles made up of two rectangles $= 4$

Largest rectangle $= 1$

$\therefore$ Total numbers of rectangles $= 4 + 4 + 1 = 9$

2. (*b*) The given figure can be labelled as shown below

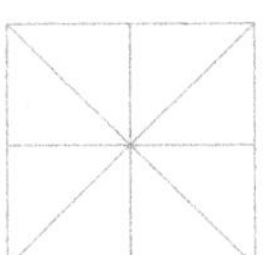

Horizontal line ——— $= 3$

Vertical lines $|$ $= 3$

Slant lines $/$ $= 2$

Total $= 3 + 3 + 2 = 8$

3. (*b*) The figure can be labelled as shown in figure below.

Horizontal lines ——— = 6

Vertical lines | = 6

Total numbers of lines = 6 + 6 = 12

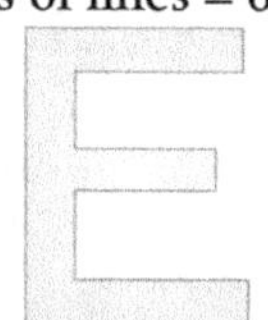

4. (*c*) The figure can be labelled as shown below

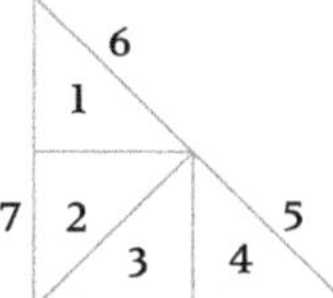

Number of small triangles = 4

Number of triangles made up of two small triangles = 2

Largest triangle = 1

∴ Total number of triangles = 4 + 2 + 1 = 7

5. (*a*) The given figure can be labelled as shown below

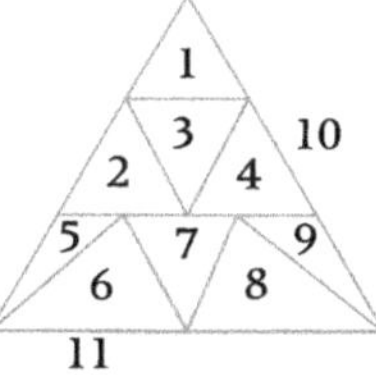

Total number of small triangles are = 9

Number of triangles made up of four small triangles = 1

Largest triangle = 1

∴ Total number of triangles = 9 + 1 + 1 = 11

6. (*c*) The given figure can be labelled as shown below

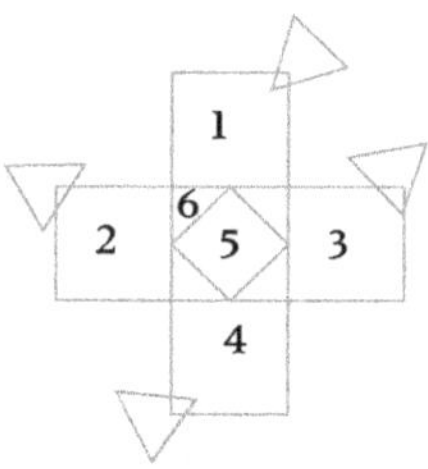

∴ Total number of squares = 6

7. (*c*) The given figure can be labelled as shown below

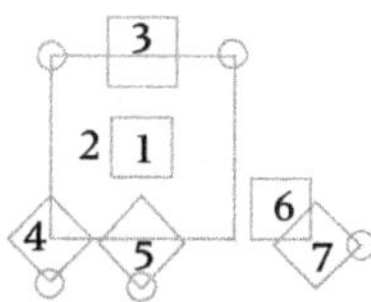

Total number of squares as we count is 7.

8. (*a*) The given figure can be labelled as shown in figure below.

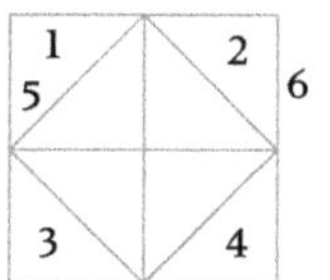

Number of small squares = 4

Number of squares made up of four units = 2

∴ Total number of squares = 4 + 2 = 6

9. (*a*) To count the number of circles in the given figure, first we label the figure as shown below

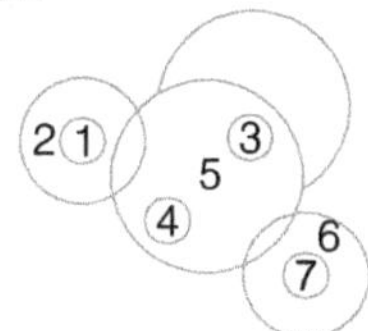

So, there are seven circles in the given figure.

10. (*d*) The given set of circles can be labelled as shown below

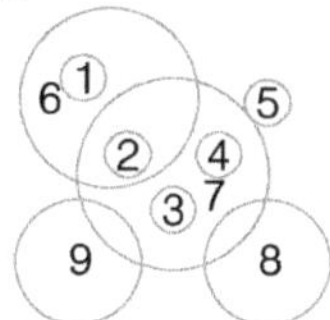

Total number of circles is 9.

11. (*b*) The circles can be labelled as shown below

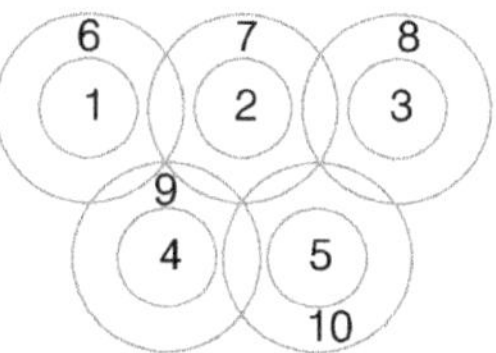

So, there are 10 circles in the given set of figures.

12. (*d*) There are four different shapes in the given set of figures, i.e. circle, square, triangle and rectangle.

13. (*b*) As we count from the given set of figures, the number of circles is 9.

14. (*d*) To count the number of squares, first we label the given figure as shown below

Single unit squares = 6

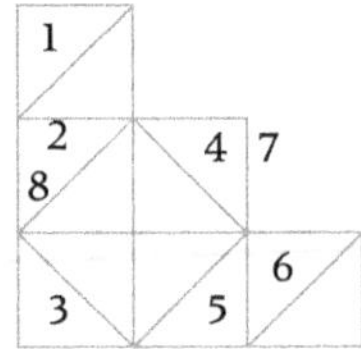

Larger squares = 2

∴ Total number of squares = 6 + 2 = 8

15. (*c*)

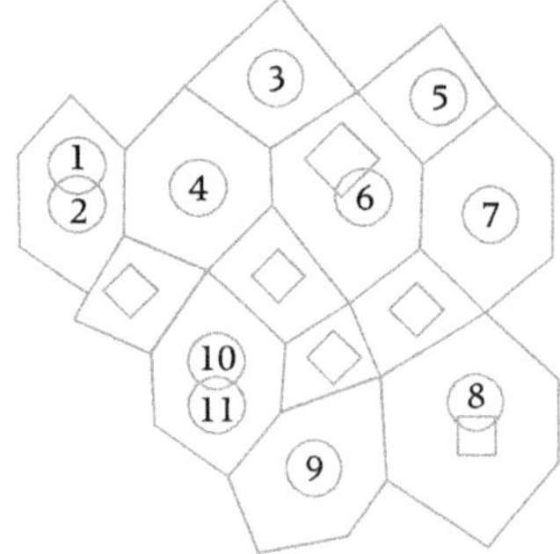

There are 11 circles are present in the figure.

9. Mirror Images

1. (*c*) The mirror image of hockey stick and ball can be seen in option (c) and it will appear as shown below

Mirror image   Mirror Original image

2. (*b*) Mirror image of Micky will look like as shown in option (b), which is as follows:

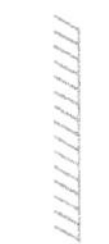

Mirror image   Mirror   Original image

3. (*a*) The mirror image of the figure (X) is shown in option (a), which is as follows:

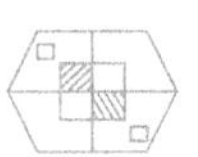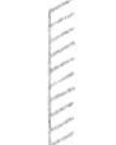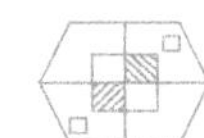

Original image   Mirror   Mirror image

4. (*c*) The mirror image of the wall clock will appear in the mirror as shown in option (c), which is as follows:

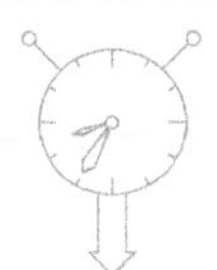

Original image   Mirror   Mirror image

5. (*a*) The arrows in the mirror of the car will appear as shown in option (a), which is as follows

Original image   Mirror Mirror image

6. (*b*) Sponge bob will appear in the mirror as shown in option (b) which is as follows :

Original image   Mirror Mirror image

7. (*c*) The picture in the mirror will appear as shown in option (c), which is as follows:

Mirror image   Mirror   Original image

8. (*d*) The mirror image of the Donald Duck will appear as shown in option (d), which is as follows

Mirror image   Mirror   Original image

9. (*d*) The mirror image of the figure is shown in option (d), which is as follows:

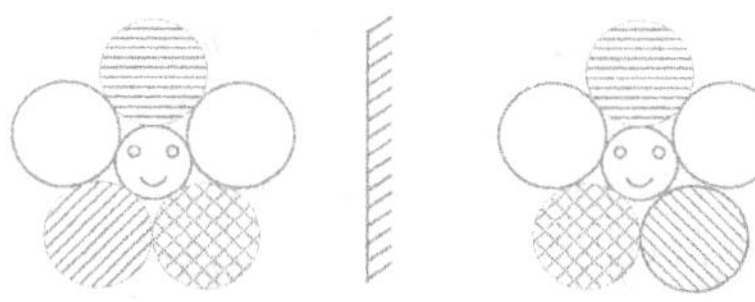

Original image   Mirror   Mirror image

10. (*d*) The mirror image of the given figure (X) is shown in option (d) which is as follows

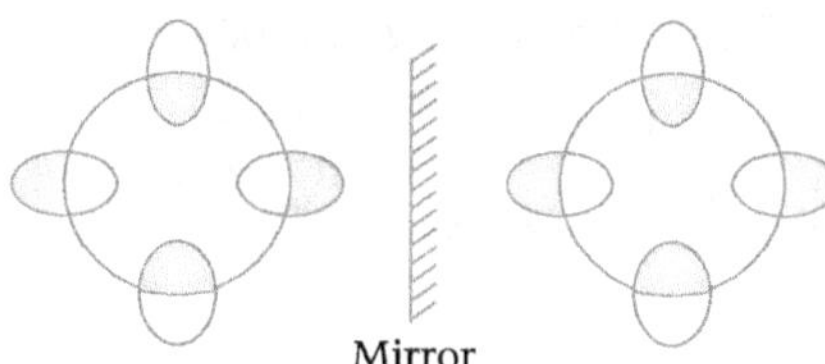

Original image   Mirror   Mirror image

11. (*b*) The mirror image of the Figure (X) is shown in option (b), which is as follows

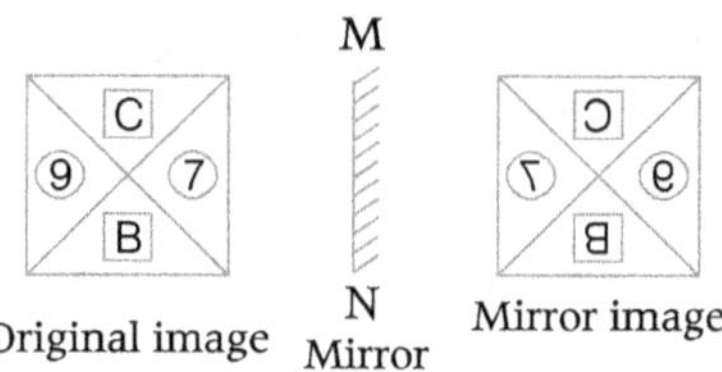

Original image   Mirror   Mirror image

12. (*b*) The mirror image of the given figure (X) is shown in option (b), which is as follows

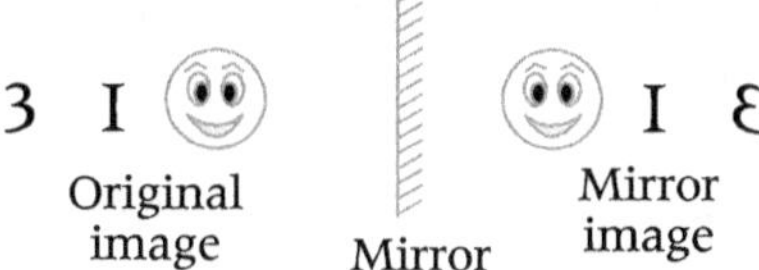

Original image   Mirror   Mirror image

13. (*d*) The mirror image of the given figure (X) is shown in option (d), which is as follolws

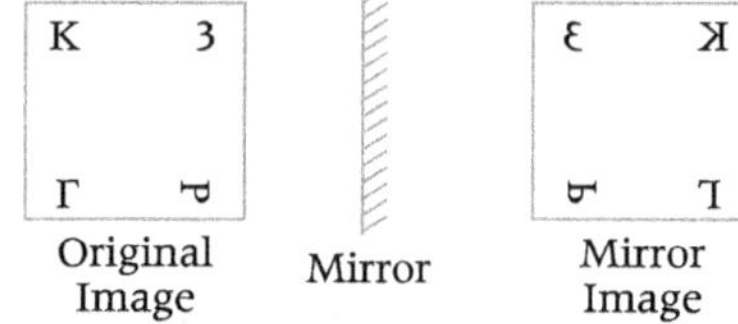

Original Image   Mirror   Mirror Image

14. (*b*) The letters of the word 'QUICK' will appear in the mirror as shown below

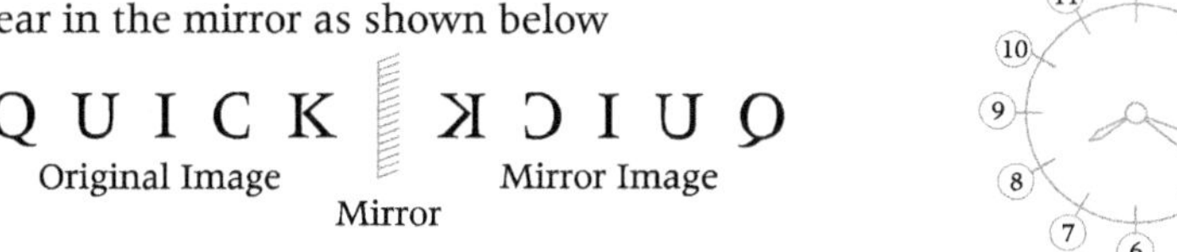

Original Image   Mirror   Mirror Image

15. (*b*) The word 'SHARE' will appear in the mirror as shown in option (d) and the mirror image is as follows

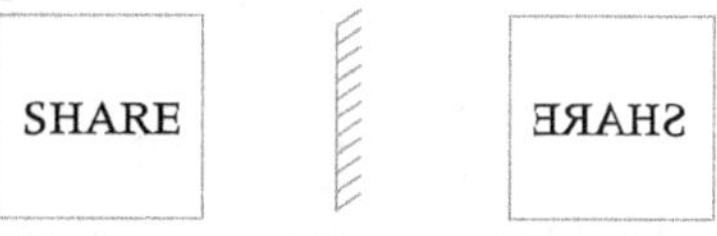

Original image   Mirror   Mirror image

16. (*d*) The letters of the word DAVID will appear in the mirror as shown below

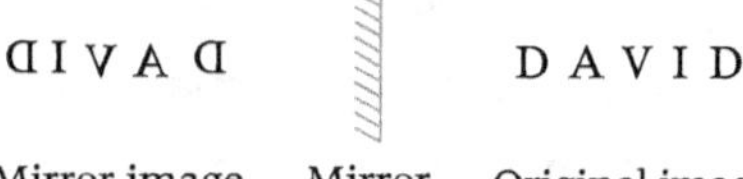

Mirror image   Mirror   Original image

17. (*b*) The number written on the wall will appear in the mirror as shown below

614932
Original image

Mirror image

Mirror

18. (*a*) The actual number seen in the mirror will be as shown below

75298
Original image

75298
Mirror image

Mirror

19. (*b*) The mirror image of the combination of letters, numbers and symbols is shown in option (b), which is as follows

←QE153→

←ε2150→

Original image   Mirror   Mirror image

20. (*b*) For mirror image of clock time, the given time shall be subtracted from 12 : 00 or 11:60. By using Simple trick we can find out the answer.

$$11:60$$
$$\underline{4:40}$$
$$\underline{7:20}$$

Hence option (b) is correct.

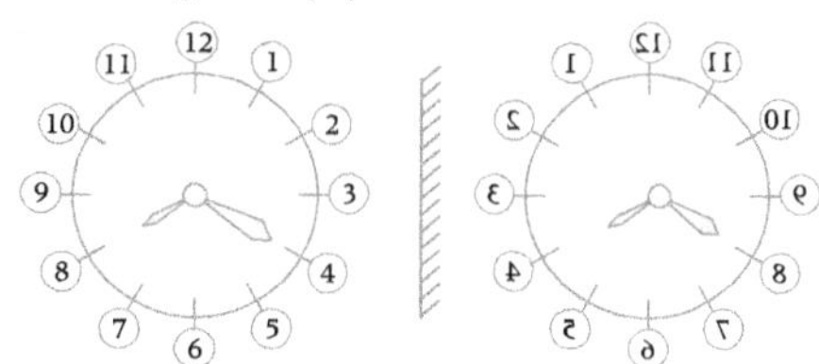

10. Inserting the Missing Character

1. (*d*) As, In row I, $8 + 18 = 26$

In row II, $\quad\quad 7 + 9 = 16$

Similarly, in row III, $11 + 7 = \boxed{18}$

So, '18' will replace the question mark.

2. (*c*) The number in the lower part of the football is the sum of the numbers in the upper part of the football.

As, $17 + 20 = 37$ and $21 + 32 = 53$

Similarly, $41 + 26 = \boxed{67}$

So, 67 will replace the question mark.

3. (*a*) The number in the middle is the sum of the numbers outside the figure divided by 2.

As, $\quad \dfrac{6 + 4 + 2 + 10}{2} = \dfrac{22}{2} = 11$

and $\quad \dfrac{8 + 4 + 5 + 3}{2} = \dfrac{20}{2} = 10$

Similarly, $\dfrac{7 + 2 + 3 + 4}{2} = \dfrac{16}{2} = \boxed{8}$

So, the missing number is '8'.

4. (*b*) The number in the upper part is multiplied by 4 to get the number in the lower part of the triangle.

As, $\quad\quad 2 \times 4 = 8$ and $\quad 6 \times 4 = 24$

Similarly, $\quad 7 \times 4 = \boxed{28}$

So, the missing number is '28'.

5. (*a*) The pattern is as follows:

As, $\quad\quad\quad 6 + 3 + 4 + 2 = 15$

$\quad\quad\quad\quad\quad\quad\quad$ [number in the middle]

and $\quad\quad\quad 9 + 4 + 6 + 2 = 21$

$\quad\quad\quad\quad\quad\quad\quad$ [number in the middle]

Similarly, $\quad 10 + 4 + 5 + 6 = \boxed{25}$

$\quad\quad\quad\quad\quad\quad\quad$ [number in the middle]

So, '70' will be the missing number.

6. (*c*) The pattern is as follows

As, $(3 + 2 + 5 + 4) \div 2 = 7$

$\quad\quad\quad\quad\quad\quad\quad$ [number in the middle]

and $(4 + 8 + 2 + 6) \div 2 = 10$

$\quad\quad\quad\quad\quad\quad\quad$ [number in the middle]

Similarly, $(9 + 5 + 4 + 6) \div 2 = 12$

$\quad\quad\quad\quad\quad\quad\quad$ [number in the middle]

So, '12' will replace the question mark.

7. (*d*) The pattern in the figures is as follows

As, $\quad\quad\quad 2 \times 3 \times 1 \times 4 = 24$

and $\quad\quad\quad 1 \times 6 \times 9 \times 2 = 108$

Similarly, $\quad 5 \times 2 \times 4 \times 3 = \boxed{120}$

So, '120' is the missing number.

8. (*b*) The figures follow the pattern

As, $\quad\quad\quad 14 \times 3 = 42$

and $\quad\quad\quad 9 \times 12 = 108$

Similarly, $\quad 13 \times 5 = \boxed{65}$

So, '65' is the missing number.

9. (*b*) The number in the lower corner of the chocolate is the sum of the remaining 3 corners divided by 2.

$\quad (8 + 10 + 6 + 2) \div 2 = 26 \div 2 = 13$

$\quad (3 + 5 + 3 + 3) \div 2 = 14 \div 2 = 7$

$\quad (6 + 4 + 2 + 8) \div 2 = 20 \div 2 = 10$

So, the price of the third chocolate will be ₹ 6.

10. (*c*) The alternate English alphabets starting from 'B' are given on the sides of figure.

So, the missing alphabet is 'L'.

11. (*c*) In each row, consecutive letters are written.

So, 'G' will replace the question mark.

12. (*a*) The pattern is as follows :

As, $a \to 1, e \to 5, b \to 2$

$\quad 1 \times 5 \times 2 = 10 \to$ J

$\quad$ (place value in english alphabetical series)

Similarly, $\quad K \to 11, a \to 1, b \to 2$

$\quad\quad 11 \times 1 \times 2 \times 2 = 22 \to \boxed{V}$

$\quad$ (place value in english alphabetical series)

13. (*a*) The pattern is as follows:

$\quad\quad E \to 5 \quad$ (positional value of E in the English alphabetical series)

$\quad\quad T \to 20 \quad$ (positional value of T in the English alphabetical series)

$\quad\quad P \to \boxed{16} \quad$ (positional value of P in the English alphabetical series)

So, '16' will be the missing number.

14. (*b*) The sum of the numbers outside the circle is equal to positional value of the letter inside the circle.

As, $\quad\quad\quad 1 + 3 + 5 + 2 = 11 = K$

and $\quad 2 + 3 + 1 + 4 = 10 = J$

Similarly,

$$4 + 5 + 1 + 3 = 13 = \boxed{M}$$

So, 'M' is the missing letter.

15. *(a)* The number inside the figure is, the reverse place value of the given alphabet in the english alphabetical series.

As,   C $\longrightarrow$ 24 (Opposite place value)

        K $\longrightarrow$ 16 (Opposite place value)

Similarly, G $\longrightarrow$ $\boxed{20}$ (Opposite place value)

11. Position and Comparison Test

1. *(c)* From the given string, it is clear that the blue colour star will be 4th from the bottom.

2. *(d)* Among eight friends, three friends are behind Leon. When three more friends join them, then there will be (3 + 3), i.e. 6 friends behind Leon.

3. *(b)* There will be three friends between Laura and Tim, when Hans and Laura interchange their positions.

4. *(b)* Ricky's and Sharne's position can be shown as

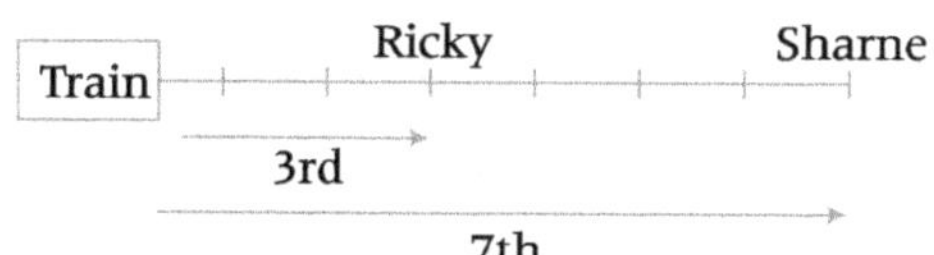

From the above diagram, we see that, there are three persons between Ricky and Sharne.

5. *(d)* Leah and George's positions can be shown as

Total number of students = 35

Number of students between Leah and George = $35 - 13 - 10 = 12$

6. *(c)* Since, Pixie is 4th from the left end, therefore her position from the right end will be 6th.

7. *(c)* Neo's position on the stairs can be shown as given in the adjacent diagram.

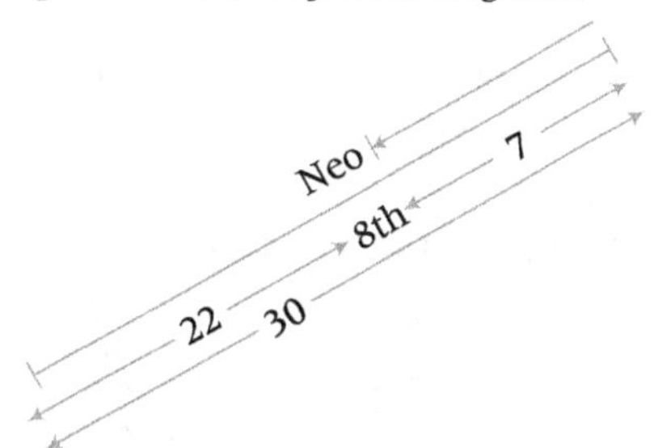

There are 7 stairs above the stair on which Neo is sitting. Since, there are 30 stairs in all, so stairs below Neo's position is $(30 - 8) = 22$ and one on which Neo himself was sitting.

Now, Neo's position from the bottom

$$= 22 + 1 = 23 \text{ rd}$$

8. *(a)* The position of Mitul can be shown with the help of diagram as

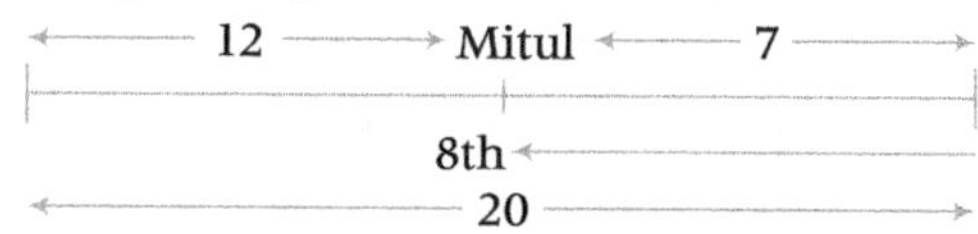

There are 7 coaches after him in which he is sitting, 12 (20 − 8) coaches before him and one in which he is siting. So, the position of the coach from left $= 12 + 1 = 13$th

9. *(a)* Bryan's position from both the ends can be shown as

There are 12 boys before Bryan and 15 boys after Bryan and one he is himself in the line.

So, total number of boys in the line

$$= 12 + 15 + 1 = 28$$

10. *(a)* The arrangement of chairs can be shown as follows :

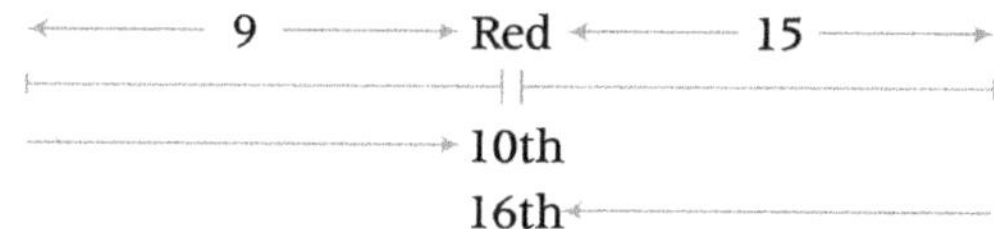

There are 9 chairs before red chair and 15 chairs after red chair and one chair is red chair itself.

So, total number of chairs in the queue
$$= 9 + 15 + 1$$
$$= 25$$

11. (*a*) Positions of Liza and Nio can be shown as

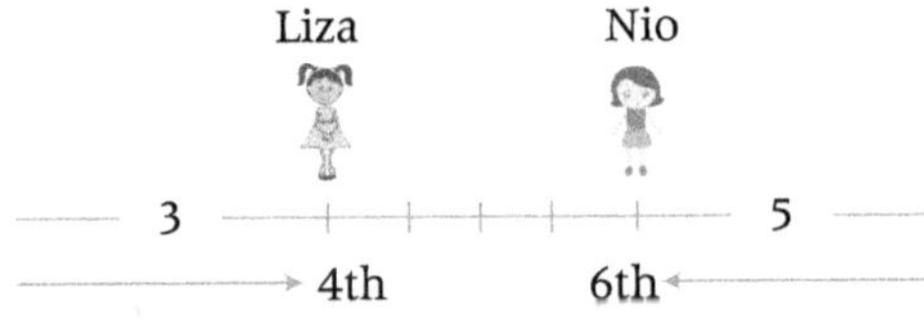

As we count from left to right, the total number of girls in the row is $4 + 3 + 6 = 13$.

12. (*a*) Persons according to their height can be arranged as

Lim > Sheena > Nami > Kian.

[here '>' denotes greater than]

Kian is shortest among all.

13. (*a*) Person according to their height can be arranged as

Motu > Priyanshi > Ashok > Jitu

[here '>' denote greater than]

Jitu is shortest among all.

Hence, option (a) is correct.

14. (*d*) According to the question,

Avani > Yami > Lovely > Gautam

So, Avani scored the highest.

Hence, option (d) is correct.

15. (*d*)

From the above equations, we get

The order from the biggest to the smallest

Hence, option (d) is correct.

12. Find Direction

1. (*d*) Marry will be in the position as shown below

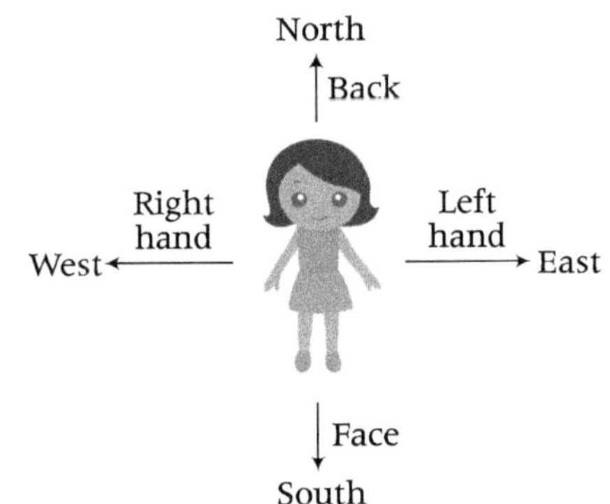

As we see in the above picture, Marry's back is in North direction.

2. (*a*) The clock can also be shown as given below

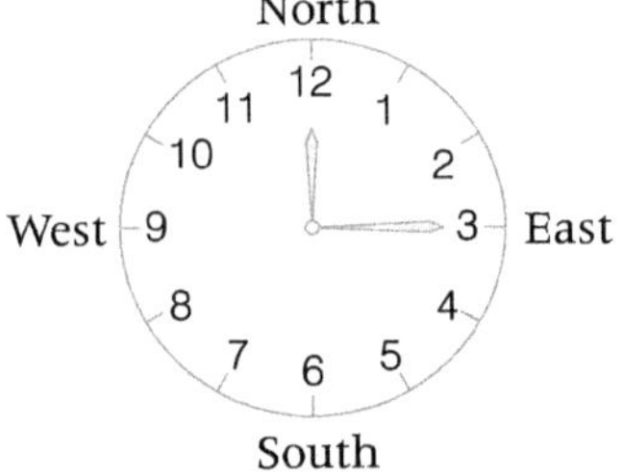

It is clear from the picture that, minute hand is in the East direction.

3. (*a*) Martin's house is to his right. Since, he is facing South direction, his right hand must be in West direction.

So, his house is in West direction.

4. (*c*) According to the question, four roads can be shown as

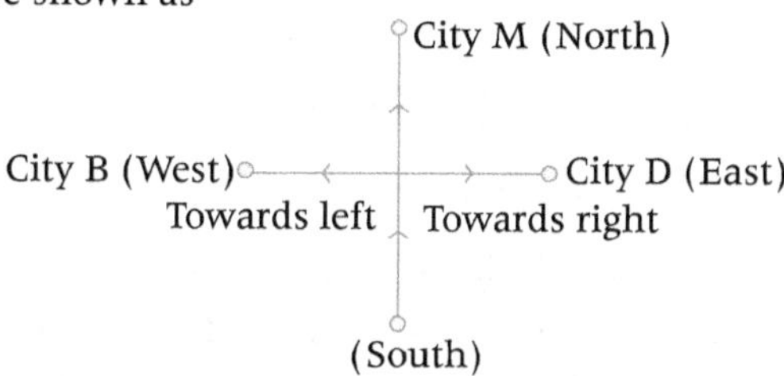

Now, we know the cities direction, so city B is in West direction.

5. (*d*) In first $\frac{1}{4}$ th turn Pranvi' will face central point, in second $\frac{1}{4}$ th turn, she will be facing pacific mall and in third $\frac{1}{4}$ th turn, she will be facing GIP mall.

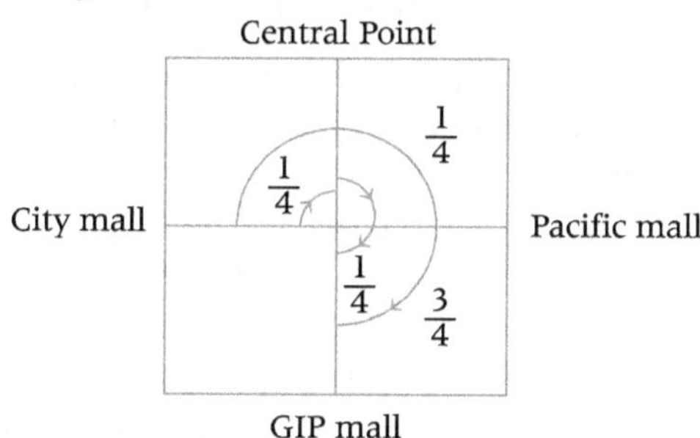

Hence, option (d) is corret.

6. (*d*) The positions of orange tree and lemon tree can be shown as

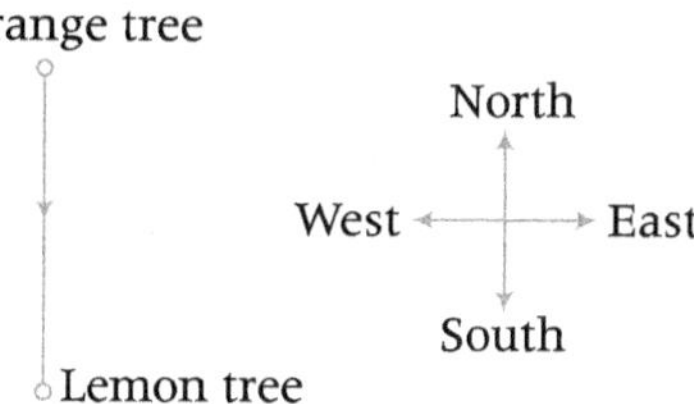

From both the diagrams it is clear that, lemon tree is in South direction from the orange tree.

7. (*c*) Since, Paul is heading towards East. The arrows on the pole depicts that St. Peter Street is in West direction and cafe is in East direction.

Now, he must go in East direction to reach cafe.

8. (*c*) According to the question, location of the different places can be shown as

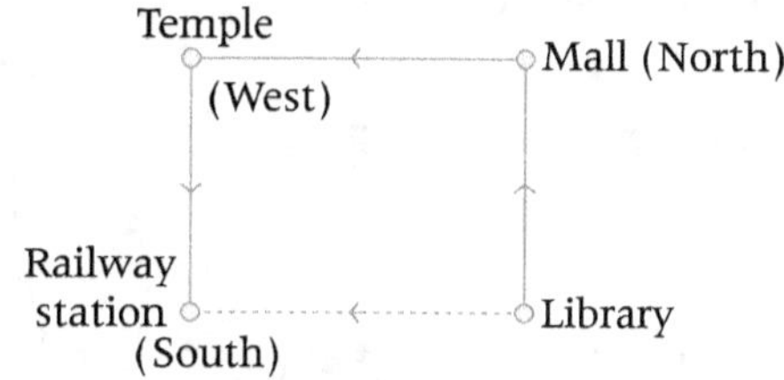

Now, we see that, Railway Station is in West direction from the Library.

9. (*b*) According to the question, the location of the houses is as follow

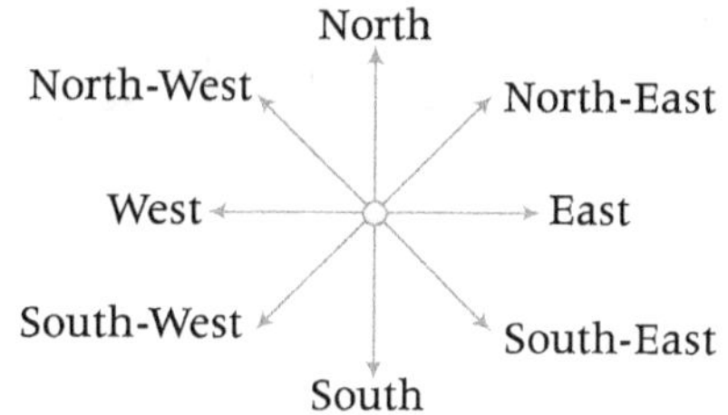

Now, when we compare it with the direction diagram, we get Harry's house is in South-West direction with respect to George's house.

10. (*d*) Sophie's house is in East direction from her School.

North
North-West
North-East
West
East
South-West
South-East
South

Church is in South direction from her house. So, the church is in South-East direction from her school.

11. (*d*) He will be facing plastic bottles now.

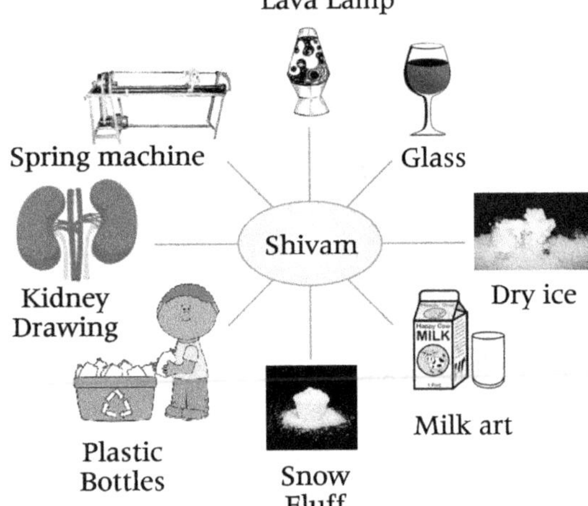

Hence, option (d) is correct.

12. (*a*) The points on the cardboard with the help of direction diagram can be shown as

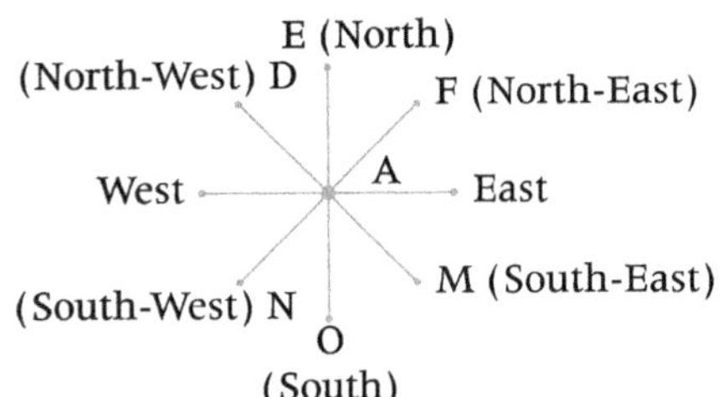

From the above diagram, it is clear that point D is in North-West direction of point A.

13. (*a*) Harper's movements can be shown as follows

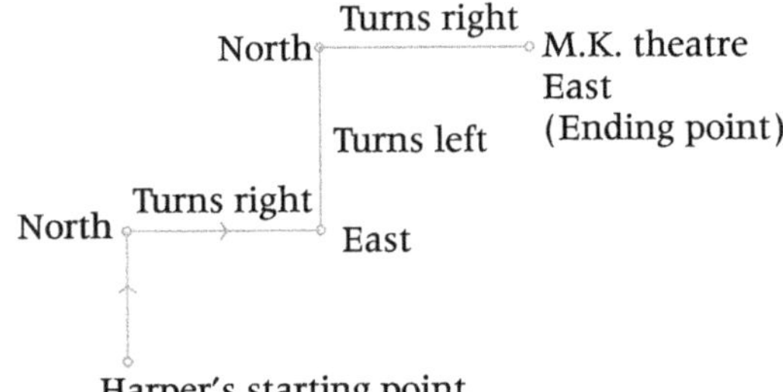

From the above diagram it is clear that, M.K. theatre is in East direction.

14. (*b*) The direction diagram can be drawn as

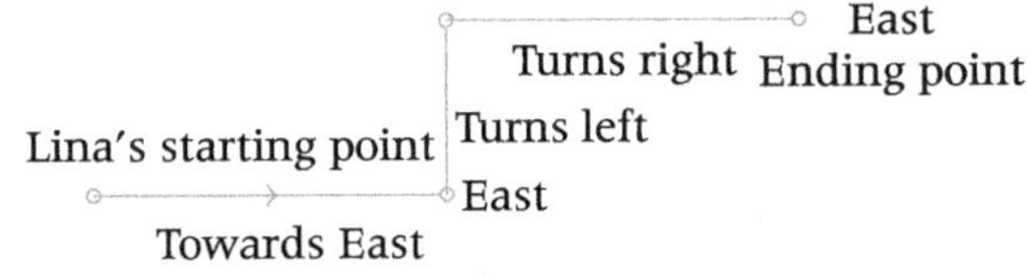

Lina is facing East direction.

15. (*b*) The movement of the football can be shown as

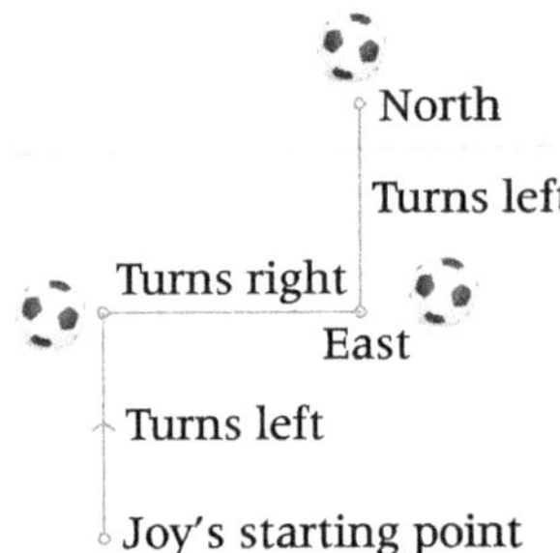

It is clear from the above diagram that, he must go in the North direction to kick the football again.

16. (*a*) According to the question, by following option (a), we get the particular path.

Hence, option (a) is correct.

Sol. (Q. Nos. 17 and 18)

17. (*b*) Cloth section is in West direction of grocery section.

Hence, option (b) is correct.

18. (*a*) Restroom is in North direction of food court section.

Hence, option (a) is correct.

19. (*c*) According to the question,

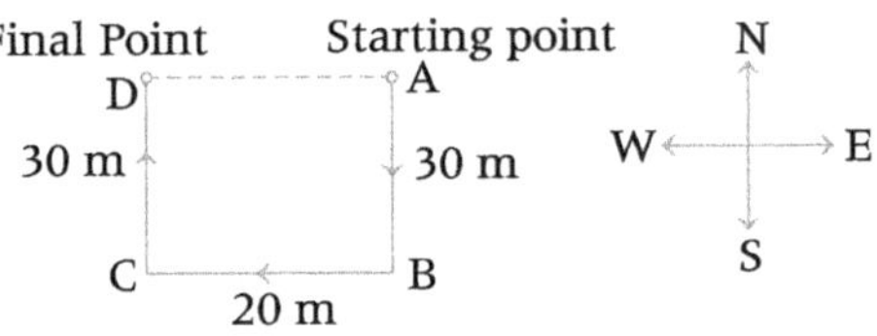

Here, required distance AD = BC = AD = 20 m

AD = 20 m

Hence, option (c) is correct.

20. (*d*) From the diagram we can clearly observe that Radhika is West to the Abhishek.

13. Calendar Knowledge

1. (*d*) The month with neither 31 nor 30 days is February.

2. (*b*) Total months would that *be* = 12×6
= 72 months

3. (*d*) If yesterday was Thursday, so today is Friday. Then 4th day from Friday will be Monday.
Hence, option (d) is correct.

4. (*a*) According to Varnika, her mother's birthday fall = Wednesday or Thursday.
According to Varun, his mother's birthday fall
= Thursday , Friday, Saturday
So, Varnika's mother birthday fall on Thursday.
Hence, option (a) is correct.

5. (*a*) Tom started his work on Sunday.
8th day including Sunday will be Sunday.
Hence, option (a) is correct.

6. (*d*) Krishna remembers the dates are 14th, 15th and 16th but his friend remembers the date is an odd number i.e., 15th August.
Hence, option (d) is correct.

7. (*b*) Total combination
Player won the gift box on monday which is 2nd day of the week.
Hence, option (b) is correct.

8. (*c*) 3rd Saturday of August 20XX falls on 20th August and three day before 20th August was 17th August.

9. (*b*) A.P.J. Kalam's birthday is on 19th of January on tuesday and after two days, the day falling is thursday.

10. (*c*) $31 - 5 = 26$ working days.

11. (*a*) There are 5 Sunday in this month.

12. (*c*) The day on which Charly celebrates his birthday is 24th October.

13. (*c*) According to the question,
Each Sunday = 7th, 14th, 21st, 28th = 4 days
Odd Saturday = 13th, 27th = 2 days
Total holidays = 6

So, number of days Gauri go to the dance classes = $30 - 6 = \boxed{24}$
Hence, option (c) is correct.

Practice Set-1

1. (*b*) Except jelly, all others are liquid.

2. (*b*) The series is as follows:
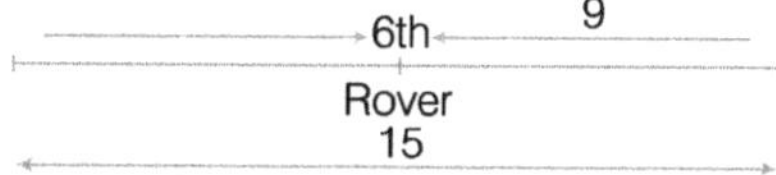
'V' will continue the series.

3. (*d*) Letter 'E' will end the first word SHARE and start the second word EARS.

4. (*c*) Rover's position in the queue can be as shown below

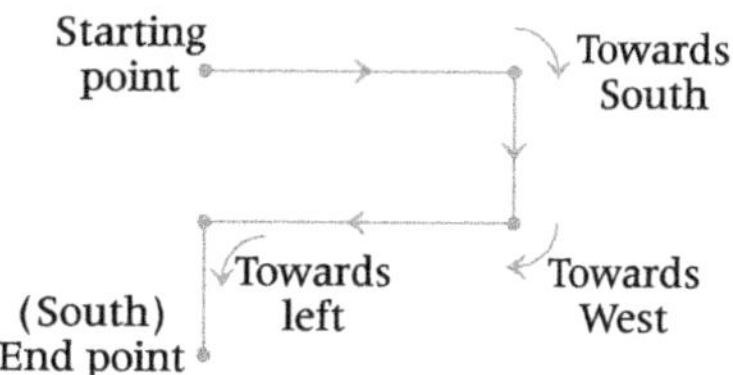

Since, there are 15 persons in the queue, there must be 9 persons to the right of Rover, i.e. (15 – 6) and Rover himself.
Now, Rover's position from the right end
$= 9 + 1 = 10\text{th}$

5. (*a*) The figure in option (a) will complete the given pattern and will look as shown in adjacent figure.

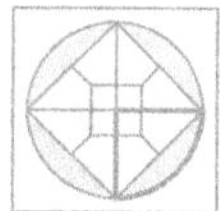

6. (*b*) The correct order of the occurrence of the following days is as follows:
Republic Day → Independence Day
    3   2
→ Gandhi Jayanti → Christmas
    4   1
So, the correct sequence of numbers is '3241'.

7. (*b*) Klien's movement can be shown with the help of direction diagram given below

It is clear from the diagram that, Klien is walking in South direction.

8. *(d)* In the first pair, the triangle comes out and the circle goes inside the triangle. Similarly, in the second pair, the circle must come out and the square must go inside the circle as given in option (d).

9. *(a)* As,

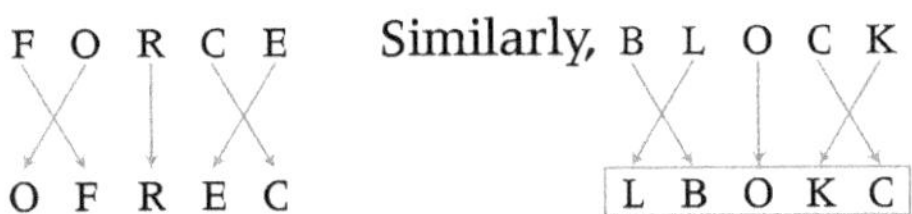

So, BLOCK will be coded as LBOKC.

10. *(c)* The given figure can be labelled as shown below

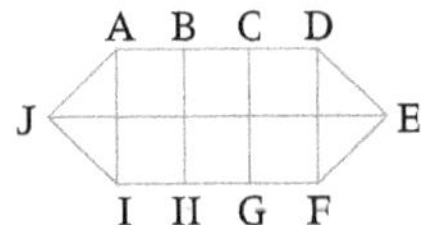

Number of lines are AD, JE, IF, AI, BH, CG, DF, DE, EF, AJ, IJ, i.e. 11.

11. *(d)* The rule is as follows:
As, $4 \times 5 = 20$ and $7 \times 9 = 63$
Similarly, $9 \times ? = 54$
$$\Rightarrow \qquad ? = \frac{54}{9} = 6$$
Hence, '6' will replace the question mark.

12. *(b)* The only word 'MOUSE' can be formed using the letters of the given word TREMENDOUS.

13. *(c)* The question figure is hidden in the option figure (c) and the hidden part is shown in adjacent figure.

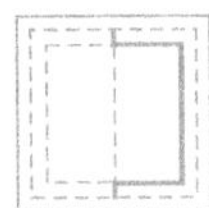

14. *(b)* The correct mirror image of the given figure is in the option figure (b) and it shown as below

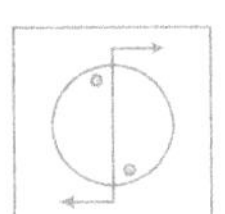 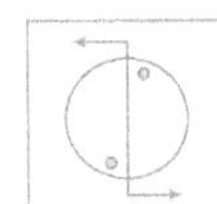

15. *(c)* First letter → A, Third letter → R, Fifth letter → D, Eighth letter → E
The words that can be formed using these letters are READ, DARE and DEAR, i.e. 3.

16. *(b)* As, $\quad$ P $\xrightarrow{+3}$ S

$\qquad\qquad$ M $\xrightarrow{-3}$ J

Similarly, $\quad$ G $\xrightarrow{+3}$ $\boxed{\text{J}}$

$\qquad\qquad$ V $\xrightarrow{-3}$ $\boxed{\text{S}}$

17. *(c)* Except option (c) figure, two corner of the each star shaded alternatively.

18. *(a)* The pattern is as follows :
$2 \times 3 = 6, 6 \times 3 = 18, 18 \times 3 = \boxed{54}$
So, 54 will be the next bogie number.

19. *(d)* Birds live on trees. But here the code for the tree is bat.
Hence, option d is correct.

20. *(b)* Sequence is given as,
A B C D E F G H I J K L M N O P Q R S T U V W X Y Z.
It is clear that letter 'S' will be eight from right end.

21. *(d)* On close observation, we find that the option (d) will complete the pattern when placed in the blank space of question figure as shown below.

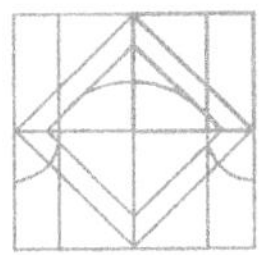

22. *(c)* Option (c) figure is not embedded in the given question figure.

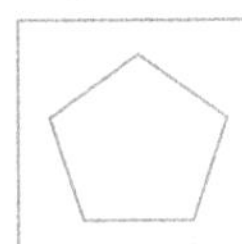

23. *(a)* The given figure can be labelled as shown in adjacent figure.
Number of small squares= 4
Number of squares made up of four units =2

∴ Total number of squares = 4 + 2 = 6

(Big one = 6) 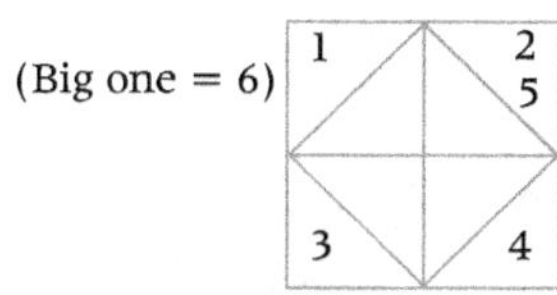

24. *(b)* The mirror image of the given word is,

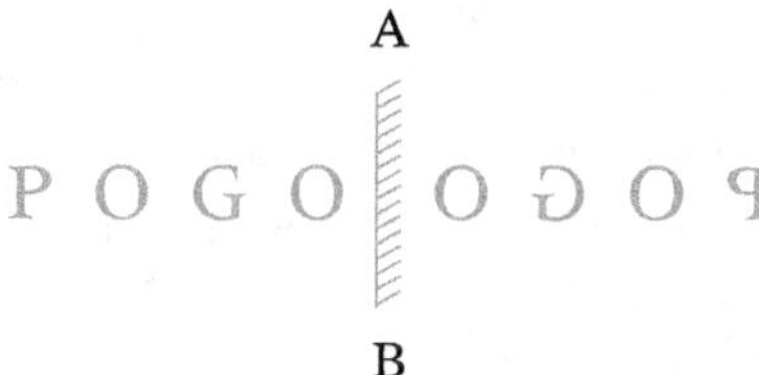

25. *(a)* Starting from 6, 6 is added in each number to get next number.

As, 6 + 6 = 12, 12 + 6 = 18, 18 + 6 = 24

24 + 6 = 30, 30 + 6 = 36,

36 + 6 = 42, 42 + 6 = $\boxed{48}$

Hence, the missing number is 48.

26. *(d)* Jiya's rank from the fitting room is 5th as we count from the starting.

27. *(c)* The clock can also be shown as given below.

It is clear from the picture that, minute hand is in South-East direction.

28. *(a)* Fourth Saturday of January 20XX falls on 24th January and four days before 24th January was 20th January. So, Sneha visiteed India gate on 20th January.

29. *(c)* As, $30 \xrightarrow{\div} 6 = 5$

Similarly, $55 \xrightarrow{\div} \boxed{11} = 5$

30. *(d)* The pattern is in figure I → 1 girl and 1 boy.

The pattern is in figure II → 2 girls and 2 boys.

The pattern is in figure III → 3 girls and 3 boys.

So, pattern in fourth figure will contain 4 girls and 4 boys.

31. *(c)* The code for the word 'MAT' is 'teo'.

32. *(b)* Except option (b) number '49', all others are divisible by number 6.

33. *(a)* In each row, the third figure comprises of a shaded circle and only those line segments which are not common to the first and second figures.

34. *(c)* The arrangement of the apples can be shown as follows :

(Red colour Basket-Apple)

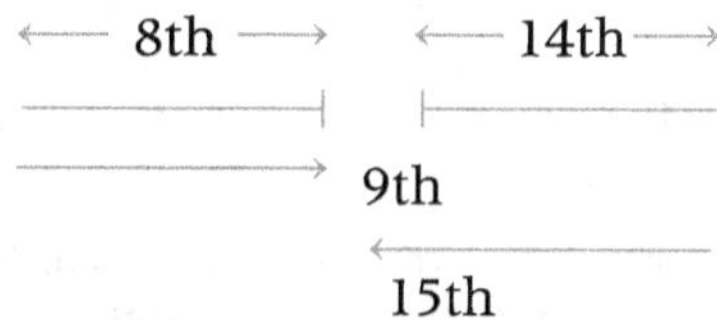

There are 8th apples before red colour basket apple and 14 apples after red colour basket apple and one apple is red colour basket apple itself.

So, total number of red colour basket apple in the queue.

$$= 8 + 14 + 1 = 23$$

35. *(a)* According to the question,

Siya > Maya   …(i)

Nikh > Kinza   …(ii)

Kinza > Siya   …(iii)

From Eqs. (i), (ii) and (iii), we get

Nikh > Kinza > Siya > Maya

Rank 1   Rank 2   Rank 3   Rank 4

Hence, Nikh got the Ist rank.

Practice Set-2

1. *(c)* Except '23', all others are even numbers, whereas 23 is an odd number.

2. *(b)* As, Mango is a fruit, similarly Red Fort is a monument.

3. *(d)* GUITAR word will be formed from the given letters and its sequence will be 435261.

4. *(b)* Fruits are kept in basket and here basket is called glass. So, fruits are kept in glass.

5. *(c)* In the given set of figures, alternatively one hand and one leg are moving together. So, in the missing figure, the left hand and the left leg must move as shown in option (c).

6. *(a)* 'L' letter should be replaced with question mark to form two meaningful words, i.e. DULL and LATE.

7. *(d)* The correct arrangement of words according to dictionary is as follows:

Bargain $\rightarrow$ Bundle $\rightarrow$ Light $\rightarrow$ Load
    2   4   1   3

So, the correct sequence is '2413'.

8. *(b)* Elina's and Jackie's position can be as shown below

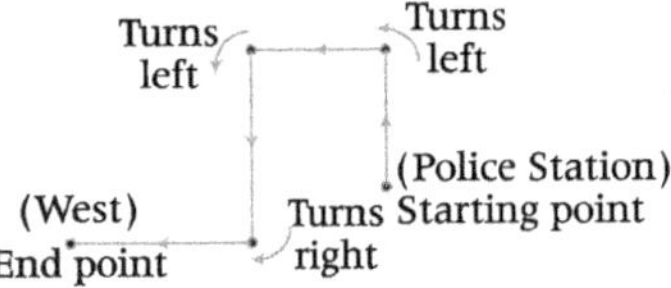

Number of students between Jackie and Elina
$$= 20 - (3 + 1 + 1 + 8)$$
$$20 - (12) = 8$$

9. *(d)* In the given pattern, in each row there are 1, 2 and 3 same elements. So, there should be two elements of the same type, as they are present in the third row, in the last block.

10. *(d)* Policeman's movements can be shown with the help of the below diagram

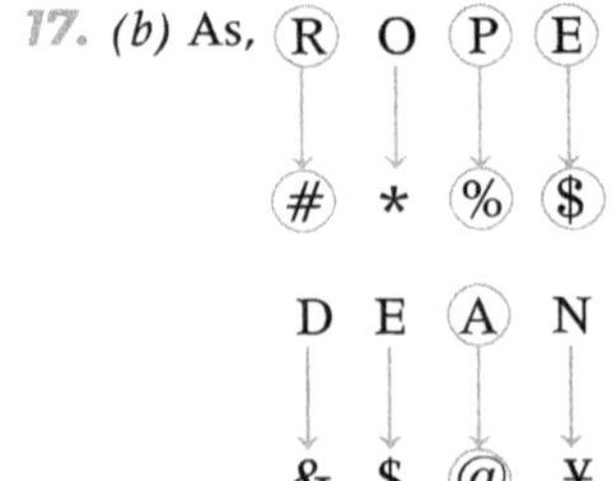

From the above diagram it is clear that, the policeman is facing in West direction.

11. *(c)* The given figure can be labelled as shown in adjacent figure.

1	2	5 (Big one)
3	4	

6	7	
8	9	10 (Big one)

Single unit squares = 8
Squares made up of four small squares = 2
$\therefore$ Total number of squares = $8 + 2 = 10$

12. *(a)* The number in the lower part of the triangle is the sum of the numbers in the upper part. As, $6 + 7 = 13$ and $8 + 10 = 18$
Similarly, $9 + 7 = 16$

13. *(d)* The figure in option (d) is embedded in the question figure and it can be shown in adjacent figure.

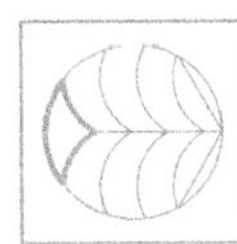

14. *(c)* The word 'TENT' cannot be formed using the letters of the given word DIFFERENT, whereas all other words can be formed.

15. *(a)* The mirror image of the given figure is option figure (a) and it can be shown as below

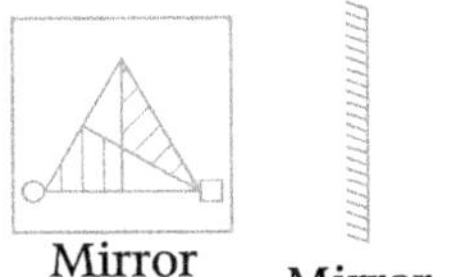

16. *(c)* As,
$$J \xrightarrow{+3} M \quad \text{Similarly,} \quad B \xrightarrow{+3} E$$
$$O \xrightarrow{+1} P \quad\quad\quad\quad\quad U \xrightarrow{+1} V$$

Hence, option (c) is correct.

17. *(b)* As,

R   O   P   E
$\downarrow$ $\downarrow$ $\downarrow$ $\downarrow$
*   % $

D   E   A   N
$\downarrow$ $\downarrow$ $\downarrow$ $\downarrow$
& $ @   ¥

Similarly, 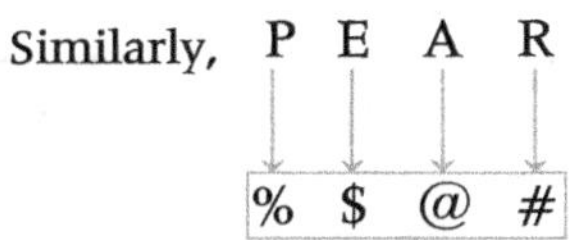

So, code for PEAR is %$@ #.

18. *(b)* All the letters pair except 'Ee' are consonant. While, Ee is a vowel pair. So, Ee does not fit into the group.

19. *(c)* In first figure, a corner is removed to get the second figure. Similarly, another corner is removed from the second figure in clockwise direction to get the next figure. Figure (c) will be continue the series.

20. *(c)* The word formed will be 'BRINJAL' from the given letters and 'BRINJAL' is a vegetable.

21. *(b)* Option figure (b) will complete the pattern.

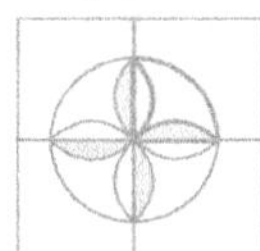

22. *(b)* The pattern is as follows,

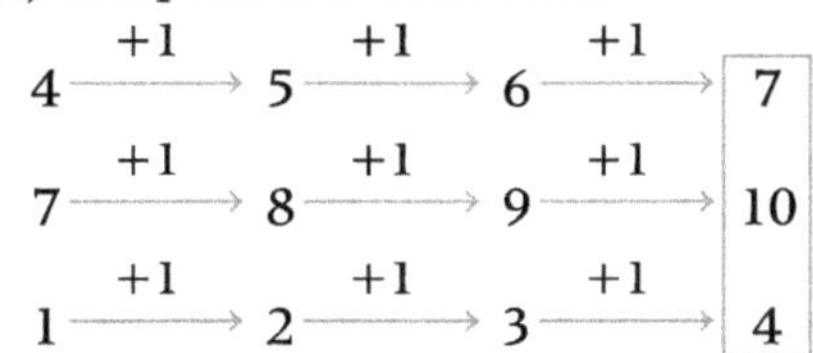

So, the last number will be 7104.

23. *(c)* As, 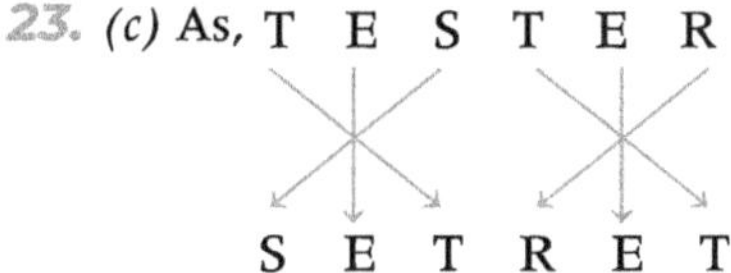

Similarly, 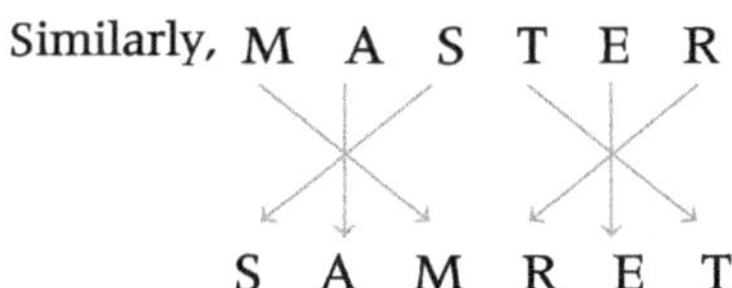

So, 'MASTER' will be coded as 'SAMRET'.

24. *(a)* Number cannot be formed because letter 'U' is not present in the given word.

25. *(c)* In each column, consecutive letters are given. So, in the middle column 'J' will be the missing letter.

26. *(d)* The mirror image of the doll is

27. *(d)* The movement of Rachna are as shown in the figure.

(P to Q, Q to R and S to P)

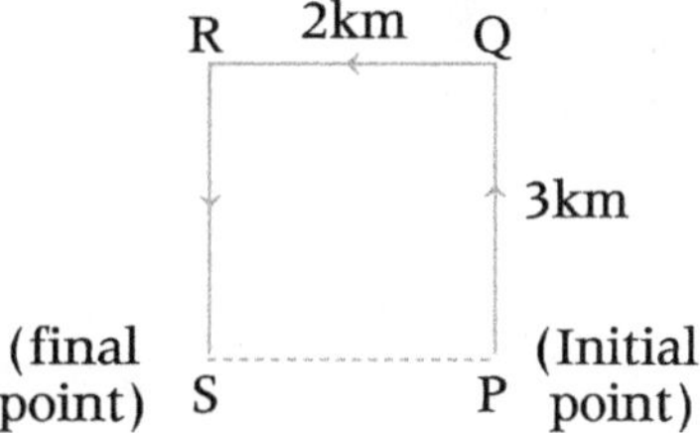

Clearly,   QR = SP

So, the required distance is 2 km.

28. *(c)* The circles can be labelled as shown below.

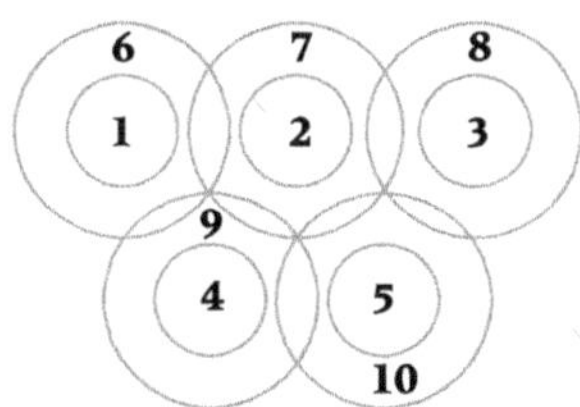

So, there are 10 circles in the given set of figures.

29. *(c)* The pattern is as follows :

As, $(3 \times 5) - (2 \times 4) = 15 - 8 = 7$
[number in the middle]

and $(4 \times 7) - (8 \times 2) = 28 - 16 = 12$
[number in the middle]

Similarly, $(9 \times 3) - (5 \times 4) = 27 - 20 = 7$
[number in the middle]

So, '7' will replace the question mark.

30. *(c)* If Laura and Suzi interchange their positions, then 4 students are between Laura and Ezak.

31. *(b)* According to sohan $= 16$ th, 17th are possible dates and according to Rakhi 17th, 18th are possible dates, so 17 is common in both cases on 17th of April, Sohan will celebrates his mother's birthday.

32. *(d)* In all the flower except option (d), the lower part is shaded, whereas in option (d) upper part is shaded.

33. *(b)* Here, 2nd saturday is on 14th February.

Three days after 14th February will be

14 + 3 = 17th February.

So, cooking competition held on 17th February.

34. *(a)* Option (a) clock will be the correct mirror image.

35. *(c)* She finally faces the club after taking three right angles anti-clockwise turns.

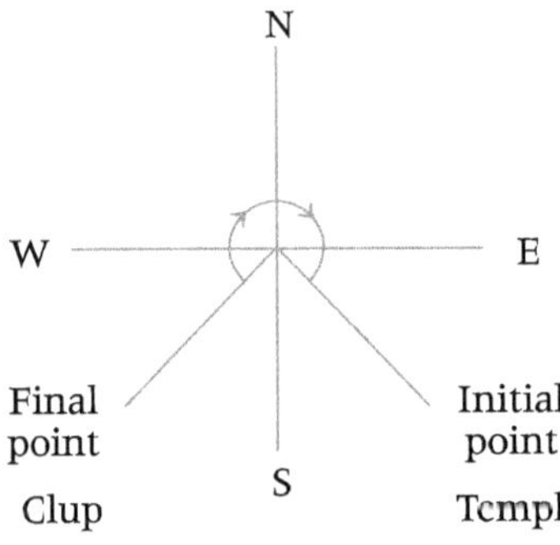